Killing Telemarketing

Copyright © 2018 Inforeads Publishing

All rights reserved. No part of this publication may be reproduced, distributed, or transmitted in any form or by any means, including photocopying, recording, or other electronic or mechanical methods, without the prior written permission of the publisher, except in the case of brief quotations embodied in critical reviews and certain other noncommercial uses permitted by copyright law.

Contents

Chapter 1:	The Opening Statement	1
Chapter 2:	Telephone Consumers Protection Act of 1991, USC 47 Sec. 227 (TCPA)	5
Chapter 3:	Let the Battles Begin	7
Chapter 4:	The First Case	9
Chapter 5:	Lessons Learned	16
Chapter 6:	The Right of Private Action	18
Chapter 7:	Catching Telemarketers	19
Chapter 8:	Spoofed Phone Numbers and Other Deceptive Acts	21
Chapter 9:	Three Basic Ways to Catch Them	27
Chapter 10:	Fictitious Business Names	33
Chapter 11:	Keeping Call Records	36
Chapter 12:	The TCPA Bans Auto-dialer Calls to Cell Phones (ATDS)	40
Chapter 13:	Consent to Call	44
Chapter 15:	Other Weird and Ridiculous Defense Arguments	50
Chapter 16:	Clear and Conspicuous Consent	52
Chapter 17:	Vicarious Liability, the "Not Me" Defense	55
Chapter 18:	Jurisdiction	61
Chapter 19:	Personal Jurisdiction	62
Chapter 20:	Article III Standing and Injury in Fact	68
Chapter 21:	The Letter of Intent to File a Lawsuit	72
Chapter 23:	Attorneys	77
Chapter 24:	Class Action Lawsuits	81
Chapter 25:	Willing and Knowing Acts for Treble Damages	85
Chapter 26:	Stackable Damages	89
Chapter 27:	Judges	91
Chapter 28:	Serial Filer Claims	96
Chapter 29:	In Conclusion	100
Disclaimer		105

Chapter 1:

The Opening Statement

At first thought, there was some reluctance and hesitation as to sharing this information. Not for the reasons some would think. There is no remorse in suing those who choose to constantly bombard us with the nuisance of intrusive and unwanted calls. Telemarketers relentlessly violate federal law daily and invade our rights to privacy with little or no fear of legal retribution. The American public should know that there are legitimate means to making callers pay for their annoying and invasive deeds. The reason for the initial apprehension is that there are more than a few bitter enemies.

The original concern in this writing is that I will be sued by those I prosecuted. Damages paid by telemarketers well exceed $100,000 and are still mounting, and I would rather not give it back.

In addition to damages paid, adversaries altogether have also incurred tens of thousands of dollars in legal expenses just to defend. None of them won, so there is no love lost. Many confidentiality and non-disparagement agreements have been signed and there are some that would like nothing more than to see my financial ruin. A handful of them have very good reason. Some had significant losses and in other cases the defendants had to file bankruptcy in order to avoid the cost of litigation and the penalties they would eventually suffer. A few might even want to file a lawsuit against me just so I have to answer a complaint in an out-of-state court as payback. This is exactly what was done to them. There are others that realize the lawsuits are a day-to-day cost of doing business with little animus, as long as they remain anonymous.

Others have written about their adventures and success stories of suing telemarketers. Like myself, most started in small claims and making a few thousand here and there. They were getting paid statutory damages of $500 per call. As my knowledge and skill level advanced, I began to average $1,100 per call, then later $2,700, and in one case, exceeded the maximum of $3,000 per call. Knowing the law and precedent-setting cases, as well as how to overcome defense tactics and arguments, can lead to successful transformation.

I am intentionally not naming past or present defendants. If this ends up being read by my respondents, some will be furious, spoiling for another fight, but this time at my expense. Some may recognize themselves in this writing and therefore be able to identify me. But if my true identity is to become known, it will be because of their actions, not mine. Unfortunately, I cannot divulge my true identity because published court records will also reveal the identities of the defendants.

The identities are not as important as the information exposed. Catching and successfully suing telemarketers can be a challenge, personally satisfying and financially rewarding at the same time. There's nothing like legally and forcefully taking money from unscrupulous callers. My hope is that readers can learn the ins and outs of the process, understand laws, precedent-setting case history and how to overcome defense arguments and tactics. In short, the anticipation is that readers learn and acquire the skills and knowledge from my experiences and encounters in actual lawsuits. If I'd possessed this knowledge from the beginning, the task would have been easier and far more profitable.

There is also some optimism that attorneys will begin to develop their skills in this arena, as too many do not; there is plenty of legalese included in this writing for their consumption. It is required for becoming successful and, more importantly, getting paid.

I am not an attorney, and I am not attempting to practice law without a license, but I know more about this segment of the law than most. All of the information comes from personal experience and research. The law provides us with the right of private action and to sue in nearly all courts. In some ways it leaves it up to the average American citizen to remedy our complaints with telemarketers through the courts because attorney fees are not allowed; therefore, finding a lawyer in this type of case is difficult at best. Once involved in this type of case, one is forced to learn and to do so quickly. My aspiration is that the information will help others create a solid foundation of understanding and inspire action to make telemarketing so costly it becomes obsolete.

In the beginning, the majority of cases were Pro Se, meaning I represented myself. Later, I wisely began working with an attorney. I have never lost a case but realized after reviewing the first $100,000 made that most of the money came with attorney assistance in federal court.

Unwanted and unsolicited phone calls are the greatest single source of complaints in the United States today. I read a headline one morning. It read as follows: "Florida Man Fined $120 Million for Robocalls." It was the Adrian Abramovich case. I read the article and looked it up on the FCC website. I found an interesting statement by one of the FCC Commissioners,

Jessica Rosenworcel. She made the following statement regarding the case: "If you think the number of robocalls you receive is going up, you're right. We're drowning in them. Last month there were 3.4 billion robocalls nationwide. That's one third more robocalls than during the same month last year. This is insane."

I was stunned by the 3.4 billion calls. I had no idea the number was so sizable. This represents over ten calls per month for every man, woman and child in America. It is alleged that this defendant made more than one million calls in a single day. Lawyers should start paying attention; there is money to be made.

I have sued industries such as travel, medical insurance sellers, search engine optimization, financial lending, merchant cash advance, realtors, heating and air, roofing contractors, precious metals dealers, business equipment sellers, solar energy companies, telemarketing call centers and more.

I perceive telemarketers as people who wake up every morning thinking, "who cares about federal law, let's dial the phones and make some money." In short, they don't care about federal law, your privacy rights or the Do Not Call registry. They are arrogant and do not think they will get caught. In many cases, they are right. I have no regret for suing them. I admit, sometimes I even enjoy it and love a good fight.

Chapter 2:

Telephone Consumers Protection Act of 1991, USC 47 Sec. 227 (TCPA)

The Telephone Consumer Protection Act (TCPA) was enacted into law in 1991 and the National Do Not Call Registry was created in 2003.

Damages defined under TCPA were established at $500 per call and treble (triple) damages for willful and knowing acts. There are some variances as to the details that will be discussed later but more than one violation can occur within the same call, so at times damages can be awarded up to $3,000 per call, whether the call was answered or not.

The law was established due the constant bombardment of unwanted sales calls from every imaginable industry in the 1970's and 1980's. In some industries, when a new salesperson was hired they were given a phone book and told to start dialing if they wanted to make a living. Home phones (before cell phones) rang constantly and something had to be done. Families stopped answering their phones and had to set up systems. For example, if a friend or family member called, they had to call, ring once, and then call back. An uninterrupted dinner or nightly TV show was a thing of the past. The law has not slowed the pace of telemarketing, however, and has by no means ended the nuisance of unwanted calls. Due to advances in technology, the calls have increased significantly. Telemarketers have become more creative in their methods and practices to disguise their true identities, deceive the call recipients and to defy federal law. Technological innovations have also increased their brazenness. Telemarketing can be a far less expensive form of advertising than print media, internet marketing, radio and TV, etc. They will stop only when it becomes more costly than other methods of marketing to sell their goods and services. My feeling is that telemarketers violate federal law on a daily basis with no concern for repercussions. That needs to change. I have been able to change the behavior of some by force of action and bankrupting a few others. Even in their best efforts to avoid legal action and financial penalties, there are still ways to identify the culprits and make them pay for their malevolent deeds.

Chapter 3:

Let the Battles Begin

Suing telemarketers started a few years ago when I finally figured out the true identity of a company that refused to stop calling. I made the request several times to stop calling, told them to take me off of their call list and even told them I was on the Do Not Call registry like everyone else.

The defendant used multiple spoof numbers, rotating or changing them sometimes and other times using the same numbers repeatedly. The sales pitch by the caller always stayed the same. I finally began to ask the name of the company and where they were located. I was eventually told the initials of the company and the name of the city where they were doing business. Other questions just resulted in lies and deceit so as not to identify the caller.

The caller was selling services regulated by a state licensing board. I am being vague for good reason; they despise me. I looked up the industry by city and business name and through the process of elimination, I found my telemarketer.

I called their office asking to speak to the president of the company and got a call back later that afternoon. I politely and calmly asked to have his staff remove my name from their call list. I explained that the request had been made several times with his callers with no result. They just continued to call. I even mentioned that I was on the Do Not Call list. His reply was to tell me that there was not a "F***ing" thing I could do about it. I was taken aback by his response. I could not believe his arrogance. I was not yelling and screaming or even raising my voice. Then I replied that it was unfortunate that he felt that way and that he obviously did not understand to whom he was speaking and that he was wrong, and I would prove it. The conversation ended. This got my ire up. I do not tolerate being bullied. I never have and I never will. I really did not care for his language, tone and arrogance. I thought a little fear of consequences may change his attitude. I had heard of TCPA but knew almost nothing about it other than there was some sort of penalty involved and that I could file a lawsuit. Thus, the first case began.

I knew that filing an FCC complaint would result in absolutely nothing. I wanted to make my opponent suffer the consequences of their actions and particularly for the company president's statements. I also wanted to force them to pay and to have the satisfaction of them writing a check. I knew that even the FCC cannot identify spoofed phone numbers because they do not exist, and the FCC was not going to financially reward me for my efforts.

FCC complaints rarely stop the violators and even when they do, they are often back in business in a week or two under another dummy corporation or assumed business name. Besides, a good old-fashioned legal beating seemed justified, given the circumstances.

Chapter 4:

The First Case

I was absolutely clueless as to what had to be done but that fact has never stopped me before, and I did not see why it should start now. I was truly a legal novice with absolutely no training. I had never even seen the inside of a courtroom.

I soon found out that there were almost no attorneys who wanted to represent TCPA plaintiffs. TCPA does not allow for attorney fees even if the plaintiff is successful. Few attorneys, if any, would take the case, and almost none have experience other than the highly paid counselors who defend large corporations that violate TCPA. Most will represent for an hourly fee and a few would work on a contingency basis. In later cases, I literally had to teach an attorney about TCPA; without his knowledge, of course, but through discussion. He would never agree to having a non-attorney teach him anything, but he learned, and he was one who was willing to hit the books and study; this was a rare find. Attorney contingency fees range from 30 to 50% of the award or settlement in this type of case. I later found that attorney fees are allowed in class action cases if successful, but that will be discussed later.

I ordered phone records from the service provider and received them a week later. FYI, cell phone detailed call records are usually available online and subscribers have the right to receive them.

But in the first case, I decided to learn how to file a case in small claims court. A week or so had passed since the conversation took place with the company president and I was still livid and determined to settle the score.

I was eager to pay the filing fee and move forward. I taught myself how to file a petition through internet searches and did so. The complaint was abysmal and amateurish but enough to open the case. It was definitely not a creation of true legal genius. The first filed complaint took up a single page; now they are several pages long. Today the original petitions are about six pages long and include sections such as a preliminary statement, a detailed complaint, factual allegations, parties, jurisdiction, TCPA, right of private action, vicarious liability, article III standing, and a detailing of relief sought.

I had never hired a process server or motioned for discovery, but learned. I did not know exactly how treble and stackable damages worked or even where to find them within the law or case law. In later cases I learned much more, like the production of documents for briefs, various types of motions, appeals, settlement agreements, motions to dismiss once paid and much more. I even learned compelling arguments to prove my case that resulted in higher awards or settlements. But for the first case, I was clueless.

In my state, the award limit is $10,000 in Justice of the Peace Courts. All I knew was that the rules of procedure are far more relaxed than in higher courts. The judge has much more leniency towards Pro Se filers and their lack of knowledge of court rules, at least for a while, until the judge later surmised that I was using her court as an ATM and making some pretty hefty withdrawals.

Like many others, I had googled the phone numbers and viewed online complaints. I also learned the defendant had locations in other states using the same telemarketing techniques. I assumed by their industry, the company was profitable and there was money to be had. I was not an attorney but I knew that internet search printouts were likely inadmissible as evidence in court under hearsay rules.

To my delight, the defendant was served a summons that started with the verbiage, "You have been sued," and it gave me a warm fuzzy feeling. The defendant's answer was due to the court in twenty-one days. Then, I waited. I did not want to be the first to call as it could be considered a sign of weakness and desperation to collect a few dollars, and negotiating from a position of weakness always results in inadequate settlement offers.

A few days later, the same company president called admitting to a few calls and offered a settlement of $1,000. The offer was declined.

I motioned the court for discovery, not that I knew how. A hearing date was set by the judge a few weeks later. The president for the defendant company appeared in court for the hearing. Fortunately, there was no attorney representing the other side. I would have been eaten alive. The judge asked what I was looking for and I responded, the phone records of the defendant. The judge immediately denied the motion stating that there were potentially hundreds of thousands of calls. I agreed with the judge and stated, "yes, your honor, I agree, and that is the problem, they keep calling and they refuse to stop and I'm probably not the only one they have called." Off to the side I saw the bailiff shaking his head in agreement as if he had enough of the robocalls himself. In the judge's defense, it was small claims court and I did not even specify in writing the discovery that I was looking for in the motion; I had only motioned for a discovery hearing. I was not properly requesting production of documents, interrogatories and admissions. Again, I was clueless. I argued that the defendant was in sole possession of the records and without them they could walk scot free and continue calling. Then, I asked the judge if she would allow me to receive a copy of the defendant's call management system records, which the defendant could easily produce, and the judge agreed. I did not even know if the defendant used a call management system but I found out that they did and it worked. I later found out that there were tens or hundreds of thousands of calls, but for this case I was satisfied with what the court agreed to. This is the work of a true novice and I left a tremendous amount of money on the table which I went back after later in another court setting—federal court—in an entirely different case with the same defendant. More on that subject later.

The defendant had thirty days to comply with the court order to produce discovery and a few weeks later I received a copy of the defendant's call management system records. The report exhibited two or three calls that were made to my phone number. I'm sure the report was falsified and could only guess as to what he was thinking; admit a few calls, pay him a little money and get rid of him. But the defendant did not realize what he had done.

I started matching call times and original spoof numbers reported on my records. The defendant intended to only admit to a few calls but records proved otherwise. It took some time because I had to convert Greenwich Mean Time to my time zone and consider that the calls were actually originated from a third time zone.

Once done, I could only match nine calls. All I knew was that damages were $500 per call. (In reality, damages could have been trebled to $1,500 per call because I asked the defendant repeatedly to stop calling.) But at $1,500 per call, I would have exceeded the court's dollar limits to remedy our dispute. Again, I was a complete novice. I knew there were more calls, but I could not prove it without additional phone records, and the defendant was not going to freely give them up, nor was the judge going to approve a new order. I was not too bright, but neither was my opponent.

I had also requested the originating phone number but only received a spoof number that was made up. He lied and got away with the falsehood.

I called the defendant with the news of additional phone calls proven. He then offered $1,500 to dismiss. He worked out of a local office, so I requested a meeting at his office to go over the phone records. I thought about the risks of appearing alone at his office beforehand. I knew that we were not best pals and would never be so. I decided the worst he would do is threaten me. The meeting ended up to be nothing more than a regular business meeting. In the document he produced from his call management system, the call times matched the call times on my phone records. The spoof numbers matched multiple calls. The spoofed number is what appears on phone records from the phone company. He then offered $2,000. I declined. He said he would see if he could raise the offer with his out-of-state counterparts and get back to me.

He called back after conferring with his partners and stated that $2,000 was their last and final offer, take it or leave it. I then told the defendant that I would file a motion to compel with the court for withholding evidence. This was a total bluff. I explained this means that the court could levy a daily fine payable to the court and in turn pay me until the discovery that was court ordered was provided. This did not seem to bother the defendant until I mentioned that if he were stopped for even a traffic violation that the judge could issue a warrant for his arrest for violating court orders. Again, I was bluffing, and I really had no idea of what I was doing, nor did I have the knowledge of how to file a motion to compel or argue it in court. The president was not even personally named defendant in the lawsuit and the court would have never ordered such a warrant for his arrest. When I look back, I cringe at my lack of knowledge. Sometimes a good poker face is all that is needed.

After some back and forth negotiations that lasted all afternoon, he paid that day. I started at $8,000 because I was sure that there were more calls that I could allege but really had no evidence as proof. I could make the argument because they attempted to give me doctored records from the beginning. The end result was a check for $4,500. They knew I had proof of nine calls. I never filed the motion to compel. I was a rookie at TCPA but got paid. I'm sure the defendant was speaking to an attorney somewhere and knew my threat was unjustified, but they just wanted me to go away without incurring significant legal fees for representation, especially if we went to trial. I later found out that they had paid a few others as well, but mostly smaller amounts. I was lucky.

The funny thing was that a week prior I had sent a letter of intent to file a lawsuit to a Florida company that cold called my cell phone once. This was a mad experiment on my part just to see what would happen. An attorney representing the defendant called me and offered a settlement. He emailed a settlement agreement the day before which was signed and returned by email and he sent a check for $500 by overnight delivery. By the time my wife got home, there were two checks totaling $5,000. It was my first payday from telemarketers. My wife was surprised, she thought the whole idea was more than a little crazy and maybe she was right. She got new granite kitchen counter tops and was pleased.

The way I looked at it was that I spent about $125 for court filing fees and process of service and received $5,000 in return—not a bad return on investment. The entire process took ninety days or so from start to finish. Some later cases took much longer and others settled quickly.

The other side of the story is that if I were really prepared and kept accurate records, the case should have been filed in a higher state court or in federal court with an attorney. I believe that there were between eighteen and twenty-five calls. Since I was on the Do Not Call list and had repeatedly asked them not to call I would have been awarded somewhere between $25,000 and $37,000 if successfully argued. Keeping records will be discussed later. Lesson learned.

Chapter 5:

Lessons Learned

There were some big lessons in the first case. Even though I have sued in municipal courts, state-run county courts and federal courts, I still get calls today. My opinion is that telemarketers think the Do Not Call list is laughable. They can't take it seriously because they would be out of business, since there are over 200 million phone numbers published on the list. There would be very few to call and besides, how many actually file lawsuits? When I get calls today I usually tell them that I am on the Do Not Call list and enter it into my call log. When they call back, I tell them that I sue telemarketers and sometimes they still continue to call. There were some defendants that were sent a certified letter of intent to file a lawsuit, had a lawsuit filed against them, had them served, and they even hired local counsel to represent them in court, and they still continued to call. This has occurred on multiple occasions. It is like free money. This is the definition of arrogance and willful acts. When this occurs, I just amend the original complaint for the additional call(s), raise the amount of relief sought and submit it to the court and send a copy to the defendant. The comments look great on a court filing or in a deposition or testimony. They were warned. It is very helpful in obtaining treble damages. Records are important if you want to make strong cases and get real awards. I usually do not file until I have accumulated enough calls to warrant my time. Six is good if you are in small claims because six times $1,500 equals $9,000 at treble damages and are within the lower court's limits (depending on your state's laws). Twenty or thirty calls definitely need to be filed in a higher court, which may take legal representation. I have also filed for three or four calls if I have identified the caller and they stopped calling and my case load was light. This can change by the strength of the case, the financial ability to pay by the defendant and how many cases I want to take on at the same time. The statute of limitations to file a TCPA case is four years, so waiting is okay, and the more calls, the better.

As a note, even though the first case went surprisingly quick, patience is a must when delving into the legal system. Attorneys and courts operate at a much slower pace than in the business world.

Chapter 6:

The Right of Private Action

When congress passed TCPA as federal law, they specifically granted citizens the right of private action. This means an individual has the right to file a lawsuit in any court, federal or state, even though it is a federal statute. There are likely many state and county court judges who are bewildered the first time they see a TCPA case filed in their court. Some accept it and others do so begrudgingly. Many may feel that a federal case has been forced upon them, especially since they are required to maintain knowledge of current law.

The right of private action is significant and unusual at the same time. TCPA also includes unwanted texts and faxes. There are other rules and statutes like the Truth in Caller ID Act and The Telemarketing Sales Rule. The penalties are much greater than TCPA but individuals (usually) do not have the right to sue. These are government actions in which there is often no award to the consumer other than stopping illegal telemarketers. It is also important to know that awards for damages can also vary from state to state if pursued under specific state laws instead of filing a TCPA complaint. Some state laws allow for greater damages than federal law permits. Connecticut for example passed a TCPA-like statute in 2014 that allows for $20,000 per violation in statutory damages.

Chapter 7:

Catching Telemarketers

Catching and identifying the perpetrator is truly the greatest challenge by far. You need to unearth an actual existent company to file a lawsuit.

Methods will be discussed as to how to identify the caller and how to take action if you wish to engage with legal proceedings. There are many success stories, books and articles written by others, but this will focus on how telemarketers operate and how the consumer can overcome their acts of deception. You will never catch all of them, but you can leave a mark on those you do. Sometimes I think I should get paid by the defendant telemarketer just for finding the loopholes, gaps and weaknesses in their operating methods that put them in the predicament of getting caught and being sued in the first place. I doubt that will happen any time soon, possibly when hell freezes over. They often can figure out their mistakes through evidence and testimony. I have seen many violators change their tactics, fire marketing directors, end agreements with third party callers and bury themselves even deeper into the woodwork of corporations so that they can avoid being identified. Almost all of the wrongdoers continued on with their law breaking ways even after being sued. Face it; dialing the phone is a much less costly form of advertising. Marketing expenses can be multiplied many times over with traditional forms of promotion. It is far less expensive to illegally operate a call center. Only one former defendant actually attempted to make a change and advertise legitimately. Driving one afternoon, I heard a radio ad by one of my former defendants.

They actually spent money to buy air time in an attempt to operate legitimately, at least for a while. I doubt it lasted long. It was probably not cost effective.

TCPA cases have skyrocketed over the past few years and damages awarded to plaintiffs have reached hundreds of millions of dollars.

Telemarketers have many tricks to avoid being caught, like spoof numbers, rolling and changing spoof numbers, intermittent or sporadic call patterns, dummy corporations, fake business names, websites with companies that don't exist or that likely have a real company behind them. Today, they are more and more likely to be calling from foreign call centers to avoid subpoenas of phone records. A company that is collecting money within the US has to be registered somewhere in order to obtain a bank account. Even if they are an overseas entity collecting funds within the country, they will likely have a US bank account and that account can be legally levied once a judgment has been rendered and certain legal requirements have been met.

Chapter 8:

Spoofed Phone Numbers and Other Deceptive Acts

Telemarketers rarely use legitimate verifiable phone numbers. Some novice callers use actual phone numbers and they are easy to find and sue. These are usually small local businesses trying to increase sales. Almost all use spoof numbers. A spoof number is a phone number that is input into the caller's call management system or phone system software. It is not difficult and takes almost no investment. In other words, the caller ID on your phone is not likely a real number, or at least a phone number that truly identifies the caller. They use phone numbers that may or may not exist. They can also input false names into the caller ID. The area code or caller location can also be spoofed. Any phone number can be spoofed and it has little bearing on the case. The call could be coming from anywhere in the world. I have seen my personal phone number spoofed. The only reason I track caller numbers, dates and times is to make a record of who called and what was said. It is important because the caller will sometimes rotate the spoof number, or use similar call number patterns or even call multiple times displaying the same number. This will become important later if you decide to pursue legal action because damages are calculated by the number of calls. Sometimes the difficult issue is deciding when to file a lawsuit or give false information to the caller to determine their true identity before they stop calling.

Telemarketers use spoofed phone numbers that cannot be identified until there is a demand for the production of their phone records in a motion for discovery or by subpoena approved by court order. Those phone records will come from the defendant's telephone service provider. Remember, the phone number appearing on your caller ID is almost always untraceable and not associated with the real originating phone number.

A few defendants seemed shocked when they learned that they have no control over their own phone records and by court order the records would be delivered directly to the plaintiff from their phone service provider. Actual phone records could easily prove tens or hundreds of thousands of calls. At this point, all of the denials in the world cannot save them. They know they need to settle, and now it is a matter of how much and when they are going to have to pay. Spoofing a phone number and caller ID is a knowing and deliberate act. Spoofing software must be purchased, downloaded and the spoofed or false caller ID and phone number must be manually uploaded and input into their call system. This will become important when discussing willing and knowing actions for treble (triple) damages in a later chapter.

Telemarketers often rotate or change spoofed phone numbers. This makes it less likely for a call recipient to identify the pattern and detect who they really are. Even if caught they think it will limit damages and make it not worthwhile for someone to file a lawsuit against them. This also avoids the issue of their phone number being blocked.

They may call in short patterns of two, three or four calls. Again, this makes it less likely that someone will sue for such a small number of calls. Sometimes they space out the calls to monthly or quarterly intervals thinking no one will be wise enough to catch them.

In an actual case, the national telemarketer only called once every four to six weeks but they always used the same spoof number. I tracked them for months and finally caught them. The case is still pending and it is sizeable because the actual seller is a well-established national seller with multiple locations throughout the US with annual revenues that likely reach well into tens or hundreds of millions of dollars.

Sometimes callers just constantly bombard you with calls repeatedly. This hinges on the intelligence and deviousness of your future defendant. If these calls are tracked correctly, you may have a case.

In an actual case, I caught one of the most blatantly abusive violators of TCPA that I have ever seen or heard. This was a company that called thousands by displaying (spoofing) actual phone numbers that were still in use by real individuals and real companies. They even displayed the actual names of the companies and individuals on the caller ID. This was done all for the purpose of not being caught and marketing their services in order to gain business and increase the bottom line. They actually thought that they would get by with their immoral acts and for quite some time, they did. One day I received a call from a phone number that I had seen before. The name and phone number was that of a small printing company a few towns away. When answered, I got the sales pitch from the caller and started to ask questions as to where they were located and who they were. This time the caller was only using the name of a logo that appeared on their website. I called the small printing office and spoke to the assistant and asked if they provided telemarketing services, which she denied. When told that someone was spoofing their number she replied that she was getting dozens of calls per day on a secondary phone line and wanted it to stop. The owner agreed. I knew the identity of the telemarketer and I would do just that. I was a bit angry and appalled as to the depth that this twisted defendant had stooped.

These degenerates are just not invading the privacy of the called party but also those who actually owned and used the phone numbers they were displaying. Let's say, for example, the Caller ID appeared as Mary Jo Smith at 555-123-XXXX and when you answer the call from Mary Jo, you get a sales pitch from a telemarketer. This time there really is a Mary Jo Smith and they are displaying her real name and phone number. Unfortunately, Mary Jo is getting hundreds of callbacks from people asking why she called. Obviously, Mary Jo is frustrated and probably has to change her phone number. When I catch these telemarketers, they will be going to federal court, which can be extremely expensive for the defendant, and they will not receive favorable treatment when they want to settle.

One of the real victims in this case was an elderly couple, the husband well into his 70's and disabled. I Googled the phone number and found the 800 Notes website where people log their complaints and vent their frustrations. It listed the name and number of the elderly couple with many unkind comments about the gentleman. I called the number to explain what had happened but since they were receiving hundreds of callbacks, there was no answer. I looked up the address on the county tax appraisal website and decided to pay a visit. We spoke for about twenty minutes and they told me that the calls had been occurring for weeks and while visiting, the home phone rang constantly. I asked why they did not change their phone number and they replied that they had the number for over thirty years and much of their family lived in Europe and it was the only way for them to stay in contact. I assured them that I would get to the bottom of it and stop the calls since I could identify the caller. The telemarketer also spoofed phone numbers of at least two other local businesses. The case was filed in federal court under a class action with an attorney. The defendants immediately threatened bankruptcy so the complaint was amended to include the directors of the company. Their attorney argued personal jurisdiction but their motion was denied by the court. Later, when they wanted to settle, it became a matter of a percentage of their assets, and it was not cheap. It was the first time that I rejected an offer of $50,000. It took guts, but these guys needed to be taught a lesson. As for me, I had nowhere near $50,000 so it was a grueling decision to decline such a sizable settlement offer, but I did. I told no one, not even my wife. That was one of the most difficult decisions I had to make. The case was finally settled at an amount that reflected a percentage of the defendants' net worth and my attorney was well compensated for his skills. As to the confidentiality agreement, I have not named the defendant. If it becomes public knowledge it will be because of their actions. I am positive that they will be furious if they read this. The signed non-disparagement agreement was extensive and included the destruction of all documents and evidence relating to the case as well as this writing and much more.

In addition to spoofing, telemarketers will set up websites that match information that they gave only to find out later that there is no business registered under that name. A website does not mean you can identify the true caller. There is no one to sue. This may not be new but it is happening more often. In order to file a lawsuit you will need to identify the company through information sources like each state's secretary of ss entity searches or by other means. I have found dresses on tenant websites like www.loopnet.com d match the fake company with the real company.

Lastly, companies that wish to telemarket to sell their goods or services often hire a third-party telemarketing company to call for them. The seller is still liable. They always proclaim their innocence by using the "not me, we didn't make the calls" defense, but in most cases they are absolutely wrong. This will be discussed under vicarious liability.

There are solutions to all of these issues.

Chapter 9:

Three Basic Ways to Catch Them

You usually cannot just Google the phone number and get the legitimate identity of the caller.

You cannot sue and get paid if you cannot identify the caller. Through experience, there are only a few ways to do so.

First, they voluntarily tell you upfront and identify themselves. This is not likely, but it happens. You will still need to correlate the information with an established business and once you do, you can file suit. These callers are likely local amateurs trying to make a buck. They are usually surprised when they are served a summons because they are clueless as to the law.

Secondly, by asking questions, and they tell you their name and location. Again, it is not likely but it has been successful on several occasions. Less sophisticated operations or newbie cold callers may give up their true identity. You can ask them to identify their company by saying things like, "I would like to know who I am doing business with" and "can you forward information by email?" Or, you can ask, "what is your call back number?" This may identify the real culprit.

Third is just to play along with the sales pitch; give false information, then receive an email or other documentation that identifies the caller. Yes, you read this correctly. I suggested that you LIE and DECEIVE. It is only fair play and often it is the only way you will catch and identify a telemarketer. Why not? They deceived you. This method has been used at times when ten, fifteen, twenty or more calls have occurred, and I have no idea about who is calling. I have resorted to this technique more than once and judges understood exactly why it was done—because it had to be done to identify the caller.

In an actual case, repeated calls were made with the usual response: "don't call," "on the Do Not Call list," hang up and so on. On the eighteenth call, I gave the caller false information. I gave my real name and email address but basically a fabricated story beyond that point. Yes, I lied.

Once done, I started getting calls from three different companies. I gave them the same bogus information and asked them to email their documents and information, and they did. The emails identified their companies. I then emailed all three a letter of intent to file a lawsuit. Within a few hours I received a phone call from a gentleman who stated his name (probably fake) and asked what I was doing because I consented to have them call and there was no justification for the lawsuit. Upon further investigation, I determined that he operated the telemarketing callcenter that sold leads to the other three firms. He asked if I was going to sue him as well. I said no, I am suing the companies that sent me their information and they could in turn sue him or name his company in their response to the lawsuit. He did not care for my response and started to scream about the call recordings giving consent and that they would bury me in court. I just caused a big problem for him and his client base, not to mention his relationship with the lead buyers and his revenue stream. I just got into his wallet, and he was not happy.

He was right about the consent and he did have a recording of the call. I did consent on the eighteenth call, but not the first seventeen. I felt justified in my actions. Being new at this I had no ideas about how the courts would perceive my deception. All I knew was that I was tired of getting these calls and it was the only way to make them stop.

At this point, there were choices to make as to what to do. I had received the seventeen calls but I assumed that I could not sue all three for the same calls, at least at the same time. I picked one of the companies and filed a lawsuit for $8,500 in the local court.

The defendant was a large corporation located in New York City with annual revenues estimated to be around nine hundred million. The defendant was served and I waited for the answer and response to the lawsuit. I received a call from their in-house counsel in New York. She offered $500 for me to dismiss the case. My only response was "no." She stated that her company would vigorously defend and hire local counsel. The conversation ended abruptly as I said "good, please do."

A few weeks later I received a letter from an attorney that was employed by a big-name national law firm that operated in many cities across the US. He was representing the defendant.

The letter stated that my case had been removed from the local court to the US District Court. A case number had already been assigned. Federal court is a place that I did not want to be. The rules and procedures were far beyond my scope of knowledge. I had no idea that removing the case was even possible and neither did the local judge, but it was. I was a little rattled by the letter and thought I was in way over my head for the first time. I was always learning something new, but this was a game changer. It was not a feeling I was used to and it was not pleasant. I called an attorney friend to help me write a motion to the court to remand the case back to the lower court with all of the relevant arguments and case history and submitted it to the federal court. The defendant paid the federal court filing fee of $400 and likely incurred more than a few thousand in attorney fees, so I knew they were serious.

I was not in a good position and had no clue as to what to do. Maybe I was just going to dismiss the case and hope there were no repercussions. If the defense's move was to intimidate a pro se plaintiff, it was working, but the tables were about to turn. On a Friday afternoon around 5 pm I received a call from an attorney. He called to tell me that the court had denied my motion to remand the case back to the lower court. We discussed the case briefly. I thanked him for the call. I called him the following Monday. After more discussions he agreed to take the case on a contingency fee basis. Besides, there was no financial investment to make, the defendant already paid the filing fee and they had already been served.

In a hearing held a few weeks later, my attorney requested the court to allow that the original complaint be amended. The court agreed since it was in the early stages of litigation and my original petition was dreadful. He refiled but this time it was under a class action in which I represented all others that were similarly situated or, in layman's terms, those who were also called.

In a later conversation between attorneys, defense counsel argued that there was consent to call and even played back the voice recording of the original phone call with my false and misleading statements. He stated that he would play it in front of the judge and jury for all to hear what a cheat and fraud I was and request an immediate dismissal. My attorney argued that there was no original consent in the first seventeen calls and to play the recording as many times as he liked and to anyone he liked, he didn't care. It was ironic to see a defendant all of a sudden turn into a pillar of virtue when they were deceived and outplayed at their own game.

Time went on, and the defense attorney billed his client for hours until a point where they knew that if a class action was certified, they could be in serious financial jeopardy. Fear of consequences is a great motivator. They began to discuss a settlement and decided to start with $5,000 and later at the original $8,500. The defendant had also racked up healthy legal fees for attorney representation; my guess is well in excess of $20,000. It is all part of the game attorneys play to get paid.

The settlement offers were denied, and they went to $15,000 and even $20,000. Still yet, the settlement had not been agreed upon. At $25,000, it was settled. The attorney literally pulled me out of the fire and put money in the bank. I assume that the defendant will be more cautious in pursuing the same course of action in the future; it was costly, and they probably could have settled the case in the beginning with me for $5,000 to $8,000.

Consent to call will be discussed further in a later chapter.

If telemarketers were smart, they would also rotate their sales script or fictitious business name. This can become invaluable once you try to put the pieces together for a lawsuit. You can allege that calls were made on multiple occasions using multiple phone numbers. When they continually repeat the same message or statements, a case can be made. Telemarketers often use fictitious names like the awards center, travel department, business services, etc. When they keep repeating or using the same caller ID, it is easier to allege the calls. When a judge approves discovery of the defendant's phone records, you can validate your allegations. I have experienced cases in which the telemarketer was very shrewd in that they only called once a month. Most people would just complain about being called but if there are records, you can make a case, whether you answered the calls or not. They still called, and it is still a violation of the law.

Chapter 10:

Fictitious Business Names

Today, numerous telemarketers use fictitious or vague company names but rarely disclose their true identities. They are quite aware that their activities are a violation of federal law and they make every effort to disguise and evade detection. The financial and legal repercussions can be devastating and yet they continue to call. Federal class action lawsuits can cost hundreds of thousands to defend and sometimes millions in damages awarded. Discovery alone can cost the defendant hundreds of thousands to identify and notify the potential class members. I have a feeling that a few of my pending cases will result in bankruptcy for the defendant. But it may also change their behavior or the cases may result in rather large settlements prior to completion of legal actions.

Here is an actual pending class action case that will lead to either a six figure settlement, a court order for the defendant to pay millions or their bankruptcy. For more than a year I received calls from a telemarketer. They always used the same sales pitch and always identified themselves using the same generic business name. The business name was a fake, of course. They originally used a specific spoof number several times but it changed over time. In total, they probably used a dozen different phone numbers. But, I could never figure out who they were. I knew the original spoofed phone number they used because of call records.

This went on for over a year and there ended up being over

fifty calls. One day I looked through old saved spam emails and saw the original phone number again, but as usual, it did not lead to my future defendant. I decided to do an internet search of the fake business name they were using and Bingo! There it was. They had put up a website to make them look more legitimate and used the original spoof number. It was an actual registered phone line. I looked through the website thoroughly to see if I could find any hints of an address, but nothing. I even read the fine details in their website, including their posted disclosure statements, privacy policy statements and terms of use, but nothing mentioned their true name of the company or location. I continued to look around and on deeply buried pages of their website and it gave examples of recordings of actual live sales calls being made by their telemarketing team members and the successful results of connecting with and qualifying a new prospect. Looking further, there was very little other information on the webpage but there was a single "like" posted on the webpage by a gentleman and it displayed his name. I started to research his name and found a LinkedIn page with his profile. But again, no address or location, not even a state was mentioned. I saw that he had posted quite a few articles and began to read. About five or six articles in, there was a memo written regarding a pricing change and lo and behold, an actual address listed on his preprinted stationery. I finally had a real lead. I then researched the secretary of state business entity search page and found the CEO, principals and their registered agent under a different corporate name than the generic one they used. Then I looked up the address at LoopNet.com and found the tenant address information matched. It took well over a year but now I had someone to sue.

The single "like" buried deeply on an internet posting and one preprinted bit of stationery was their downfall. Time and patience and a single small thread of information led to identifying the deviants. They were finally caught after all of their efforts to shroud their true identity.

The point is that keeping call records is essential. The willingness to do a little digging and research can pay off handsomely.

Chapter 11:

Keeping Call Records

The first case taught the lesson that call records are priceless. They are not proof but can be very important to building a case. I have found no other way to remember calls, dates, times, conversations, identifying verbiage, sales pitch or pre-recorded messages. These are extremely important in determining to file a lawsuit and for how many calls you can allege and what you might receive in damages or settlements. When a caller continually repeats the same information or recording time and again, it is easy to allege the complaint, even if they use different spoof numbers. If accurate records are kept, you may find not just two or three calls but possibly several calls even over long periods of time. Damages can build exponentially. You can honestly testify as to your allegations. It will be up to the defendant to prove you wrong with evidence of their phone records. This would be rare because the defendant usually denies calling you in the first place. I have at times under filed and found more calls later after discovery. I like to keep my reputation with the court intact.

I usually don't file lawsuits or send letters of intent to sue for just a few calls. I wait and let them continue to call; the more the better. Again, like hunting, it takes patience. Many callers will cap the number of calls to limit their potential liability. Many stop after three or four calls. It is a difficult decision as to when to pull the trigger and file a lawsuit or consent to gain information. Sometimes they just stop calling for at least a period of time. If you have records you can go after them once they restart calling again.

This happened when a local realtor kept calling. I don't think they were aware of TCPA and the potential liability that they were incurring. The caller was a newbie real estate agent that was licensed for less than a year. I'm sure he could not afford the advertising expenses like more experienced successful agents, so he smiled and dialed. I called the office and spoke to the receptionist advising her about TCPA and to bring it to the attention of the broker or manager. The receptionist did not seem to understand. I had enough calls to sue but did not. I passed by their office on a regular basis so one day I stopped in and spoke to the receptionist. Again, she did not understand. I asked for a manager and she said that I would have to make an appointment and if I wanted to address the realtor group that I would be required to pay $150 annual fee to become a preferred vendor and once a year I would have the opportunity to speak to the group and, of course, provide a lunch for the members. She was the gatekeeper and realtors seem to view themselves as substantial influencers to local economic activity. They are bombarded by callers such as title companies, mortgage lenders, handymen, appraisers, etc. They all seek realtor referrals and are willing to pay to get them. I advised her that I had no interest in her group or paying $150 to speak to them and that I was offering some advice as to how to avoid financial loss. She really did not grasp the concept that I or someone else could legally and forcibly take their money for the unwanted calls. I handed her a business card and asked her to pass it along to the manager if she had any questions. I left and they were warned.

The calls stopped for nearly a year and then started again. It was the same office and the same sales agent. I sued in small claims for both the original calls and the more recent calls. They hired an attorney to defend. I few months went by and their attorney finally convinced his clients that the calls were a serious violation of federal law and they would end up paying.

They settled prior to discovery for $4,200. My mistake is that I settled too reasonably. But it was early into my second year of suing telemarketers so I was happy to take the check and move on. The real question was who was going to pay, the broker overseeing the real estate agent or the agent making the calls? FYI, each state has a real estate commission or a realtor association or both. This is a good source to look up agents, offices and their managing brokers. In this case, I named the broker as the defendant and listed that agent as the caller.

The point of the last case is that catching telemarketers takes perseverance. You must observe your target in order to catch them. I keep an Excel spreadsheet on my computer. Someone should develop a user friendly phone application. There are other ways to get the same result but it is imperative to keep records. I log all unknown calls. It does not take a lot of time and sometimes I do not log them until I have time. The only records I keep are date, time, caller's phone number and comments. All are critical but comments are the most important. I note if it was to my cell or home phone. I also note if it was a live person or a prerecorded phone call. Also noted is the verbiage used in a sales pitch. Notes can include if the caller responded or there was dead air. This is a possible way to detect if there was the use of an auto-dialer. This subject will be reviewed later when assessing damages.

These are important as to how the case will be filed and as to what specific violations of TCPA can be alleged. Prerecorded calls to cell phones are specifically prohibited under TCPA and may be grounds for a class action or greater damages. Additional damages can be awarded for each violation even though it was within the same call. Also noted is what I told the telemarketer such as being on the Do Not Call list or "I sue telemarketers." That is a pretty powerful statement when filing a complaint or presenting to a jury and when seeking treble damages for willful acts. It also makes defendants more likely to settle quickly and for a higher amount.

Sometimes calls are unanswered. These calls are not likely to appear on the detailed call records from the phone service provider. I usually take a screenshot for my records. They will become important evidence later if there is a trial. Too many times I hear complaints from others about telemarketers but they can never prove how many times they were called and from what numbers. If you want to be successful in suing telemarketers you need to keep track of their calls.

Chapter 12:

The TCPA Bans Auto-dialer Calls to Cell Phones (ATDS)

This subject includes some legalese but it is extremely important in determining and obtaining damages.

There is a potential difference when there is use of an auto dialer in regards to the amount of damages awarded. Calls in violation of the Do Not Call registry are up to $500. Calls using an auto-dialer to a cellular phone have statutory damages of $500. There is no judicial discretion as to the amount of the award. Treble damages still apply in both instances for willful and knowing conduct by the defendant.

The following is a recital in a TCPA complaint addressing prerecorded calls to cell phones.

The TCPA bans persons and entities from initiating telephone calls using an automated telephone dialing system (or "auto-dialer") to any telephone number assigned to a cellular telephone service unless prior express consent has been given. See 47 C.F.R. § 64.1200(a)(1)(iii); see also 47 U.S.C. § 227(b)(1).

FCC rules originally defined an automatic telephone dialing system (ATDS) as, "equipment that has the capacity to (a) store or produce telephone numbers to be called, using a random or sequential number generator; and (b) to dial such numbers."

Due to advancements in technology the FCC later ruled an ATDSas,"equipment which has the capacity to dial without human intervention."

The use of an auto-dialer is somewhat difficult to prove without subpoenas, discovery and depositions. Defendants often lie as to their answer to the complaint and in initial discovery. This has happened with signed affidavits, testifying to the truthfulness as to their answers. I won a case basically because of the untruths stated by the defendant in almost all areas of interrogatories, admissions and even their original answer to the lawsuit. The defendant refused to verify his answers without a court order and could not appear for the trial because of potential perjury charges. His attorney finally convinced his client that he would lose and to pay the full settlement amount. He was wise because he avoided travel expenses as well as additional legal fees. The process took some months to resolve but I had refused to accept lesser offers to close the case and the defendant begrudgingly decided to pay up. This defendant was arrogant and thought he was untouchable. The only disappointment is that he did not have to pay more.

I explained to a judge regarding the use of an auto-dialer in this way. There are only three ways to call someone. First is to manually press the digits on the phone. The second occurs with the use of a CRM (Customer Relationship Management) software. In this case a number may appear on the caller's computer screen along with other information like name, address, email, etc. There are CRM systems like Salesforce that have features like "click to call" or "lightning dialer." When the caller clicks the phone number on the computer screen the system dials the call recipient, connects and the caller speaks, selling their product or service. This is a direct connection and there is no pause or momentary delay. This is technically not the use of an ATDS because it involves human intervention. The defendant in the case could not respond because they denied the use of even a CRM based call and stated that the staff manually dialed each call.

The third way is the actual use of an auto-dialer in which five, ten or fifty or more telemarketers working in a queue are signaled when there is a call connection and then they pick up and sell. Often times the auto-dialer gets ahead of the callers causing a delay or there is no one available to speak when you answer the phone resembling being put on hold. The difference is that with the use of a CRM the caller wants to speak immediately and can respond immediately to the answered call. With the use of an auto-dialer that is not always true, technically the calls are being put on hold until the caller is signaled that there is a connected call and begins to speak. There was another case when giving testimony in a default judgment hearing, I told the judge that I believed that an auto-dialer was used because most of the first nine calls were answered but no one responded and all I heard was dead air. It was also helpful that I could prove that there was a single caller assigned to call campaign and that the calls were originating from the Philippines. It made sense to the judge that the caller could not keep up with the auto-dialer and he awarded in my favor for two violations occurring in the same call. This first was for the Do Not Call violation and the second for the use of an auto dialer. Note that all judges may not come to the same decision and in some cases of precedent rulings went the opposite way. How this is represented and argued makes the difference in damages awarded. This was an unusual case in which a foreign telemarketing firm was calling for an east coast business equipment supplier.

In the case just mentioned, I had sent the company CEO a letter of intent to file a lawsuit. He called and apologized profusely. He said that he had hired a Filipino company because they promised cheap results. Filipino companies pay their average call center employee the equivalent of about five hundred US dollars a month and this particular company billed at a rate around $6 per hour for telemarketing services.

He stated that he was just looking for a cheap way to find prospects to sell. He also proclaimed he hated telemarketers himself and only did it because his business was failing; he had a twenty-year-old vehicle and lived in a rented house. He said he was flush with cash back in the 80's and 90's but even if he were sued there was nothing he could pay. Again, he apologized repeatedly. I asked if he had the name of the telemarketing firm that he had hired, and he replied, "yes, as a matter of fact I have emails and invoices and can forward the information to you now if you like." He did. The emails contained the company name, specific individuals, a US address and invoices for services with payment instructions to a US bank. The bank name and location was a key to pursuing a foreign telemarketer. I knew if they did not respond to the lawsuit that at least the bank account could be levied. This was all of the proof that I needed to prove my case. Being skeptical of the CEO's true financial status but not heartless, the man was never named in a lawsuit. I took his continual apologies into consideration. If he were lying, he was good and should get an award for his performance. I left him alone and sued the telemarketer. The telemarketing company never answered the lawsuit, defended or appeared, thus a default judgment. I went after their bank account after the judgment was rendered by the court. Making the second $100,000 appears to take a little more work than the first and presents a few more challenges.

Chapter 13:

Consent to Call

Defendants will use some type of "consent to call" argument in an attempt to have a lawsuit dismissed.

By statute, telemarketers are allowed to call if they have your permission or what is legally known as "prior written consent to call" or an "established (business) relationship." Telemarketers are allowed to call once in a twelve month period to a residential phone line without violating TCPA, but if the caller continues to call within the twelve month period, the first call can retroactively be alleged as a violation. A single call to a cellular phone is a violation.

Others are allowed to call as well, such as political groups, emergency calls, nonprofit organizations, charities, legitimate survey companies, limited types of medical related calls and others with which you have an established relationship. Note that some telemarketers will disguise themselves as a survey company in an attempt to avoid reprisal. If the caller is selling or promoting a specific product or service, they are a telemarketer and subject to penalties established by law.

Established relationships do not last forever. Six to twelve months since you have done business may be interpreted as no longer giving consent to call. For example, just because you had auto repair done two years ago, that does not mean that the repair shop can cold call and attempt to schedule new service. If you have someone that continues to call, tell them that they no longer have consent to call and make a note.

If they continue to call, send a certified letter of revocation, revoking consent to call. That usually does the trick, but if they don't stop calling, you have proof and a stronger case. Revocation of consent is taken seriously by the courts. It may be well worth the cost of certified mail.

Previously discussed was a case in which I consented on the eighteenth call but not the first seventeen calls and blatantly deceived the caller. The way I look at it is they were attempting to deceive me first with their nuisance calls. Telemarketers operate in such a deceptive manner that there is no other way to catch them or it would leave TCPA null and void. It would be a free-for-all for telemarketers. Sometimes you have to fight fire with fire. The deceptive acts have resulted in tens of thousands in settlements.

I have heard of others who invite local services companies that tele-market (such as solar, heat and air, alarm companies, water delivery, etc.) to their homes for an appointment, get a business card to prove their cases and file lawsuits. Mostly these are small cases where the called party is looking for smaller awards or settlements from local companies that violate TCPA. I have never tried this but this a way to determine the identity of the telemarketer or the company that they represent.

In another actual case, the defendant's attorney answered my letter of intent to file a lawsuit with strongly worded allegations of blackmail and extortion. The following is the actual verbiage used in the defense attorney's letter.

"As a preliminary matter, please know that your letter constitutes actionable extortion barred by state laws. It is a violation of Penal Code Title 7, Chapter 31, to threaten to initiate legal proceedings against a person or entity unless money is paid to you."

"Commonly called 'blackmail,' this is an unlawful practice that is actionable and permits a victim of extortion to bring claims of civil extortion, namely, being threatened with legal action unless a sum of money is paid."

"My client does not take threats lightly and your demand is both overstated in substance and unfounded in its aggression. Should you choose to initiate a lawsuit against my client, please know that we will file a counter claim lawsuit against you for civil extortion."

At first, this type of threat and allegation can make you rethink your case and cause some loss of sleep. This has occurred more than once. It is just another attorney attempting to intimidate. Nowadays, I pay no attention to their bullying tactics and don't give it a second thought other than to remember it when negotiating a settlement. These tactics usually result in an additional cost to the defendant.

The letter continued, stating that I had consented to the calls and that I had engaged in a series of webpage clicks, affirmatively opting in to marketing emails, opening them and specifically authorizing contact.

None of this was true and, even if true, it does not constitute consent to call. I had never heard of the defendant until they started to call nor had I received emails or entered their website. They declared that the lawsuit was not actionable and consent to call had been well established. After all of the threats, the last paragraph offered a settlement of $500 to dismiss the case and go away.

I knew if this was their best argument, they wou[ld] however, research their website at a later date bu[t] I decided to move forward with the lawsuit. This was defendant that was warned on the first call not to call [it]. They later even stated so, admitting one call in their origi[nal] answer to the lawsuit.

I did not respond to the letter and just filed the lawsuit. I saw no sense in arguing a $500 offer. Once served, the defense attorney called, furious that I did not respond to her letter. I replied, "I did respond, I filed the lawsuit." She stated that she was appalled by my behavior and it never would have occurred to her that I would react in such an unconscionable manner. I thought it was amusing and relished her anger. I considered it payback for her threats of filing a countersuit for blackmail and extortion. I wondered if it was worth filing a state bar association complaint against her for her statements. Her client had been served and she in turn filed her answer with the court with a twelve page document. It was quite a spectacle of legal writing and included a list of all of my past and present cases as to insinuate that I was a serial filer and therefore the case was frivolous and should be dismissed. I doubt the well-crafted legal document was even read by the judge.

This was another out-of-state defendant and I knew they were going to have to hire a local attorney. TCPA defense attorneys are far and few between and none of them are cheap. It would cost more than a few thousand to defend. I emailed the attorney a copy of my phone records but nothing more. A pretrial hearing was scheduled a few months out, so I waited. I knew I would eventually hear something. I was requesting damages of $6,000. The funny thing is that my name was never removed from their call list and they continued to call, it. This arises more often than one sought now became $7,500.

etrial hearing, the attorney called. more cordial. I knew she wanted to discuss a settlement. This told hired local counsel to appear. She to dismiss and I just said no. As a usual tactic, she asked, what would you take? Never answer that particular question. It is a trap. I in turn inquired about the limit that her client authorized for settlement. She said that she was not authorized to settle at any certain amount and again asked what I would take. I thought to myself, why am I negotiating if she has no authority to settle? I told her that I was not willing to negotiate with myself and the damages of $7,500 stood firm. She was attempting to limit the damages. A lot of money has been won and lost by a few misspoken words during negotiations or even the appearance of weakness. It is a lesson learned long ago and readers that find themselves in this situation need to pay close attention. She then stated that she would get back to her client. She was being nice this time and she knew that I would not react well to threats. She had learned her lesson and she was trying to settle for as little as possible. She was just doing her job. We negotiated over a few phone calls and she informed me that the defendant was already paying her quite a sum for her legal representation and he was not getting off without financial consequences. And, of course, she threatened in a nice way that she would hire counsel to appear in court and she could spend her client's money that way. But I knew if she could, she would have already done so. Again, few attorneys are well versed in TCPA and those that are come at a cost.

Remembering her claims of extortion and blackmail, there was a price to pay for her arrogance. It would be paid by her client, but I didn't really care. I finally articulated that $6,000 makes the case go away and we would be finished. She agreed with no counter offer. I really did not want to appear in court either. At issue was the hearing in a few days and we needed a settlement agreement and a check prior to the hearing. I was hesitant to dismiss a case with a check from a disgruntled defendant. I would need time for the funds to clear but was not afforded that luxury. The attorney offered to have a check from her law firm sent overnight and delivered first thing in the morning. It has been my understanding that there are financial requirements that law firms must comply to, so a check from her law firm was fine. To close, the settlement agreement was finalized, funds paid and a motion to dismiss with prejudice was filed with the court a few hours before the hearing.

Chapter 15:

Other Weird and Ridiculous Defense Arguments

Attorneys do not think like the rest of the human race. Maybe some of it is by nature but much of it is trained in law school. They are an odd bunch, but they have to be appreciated.

A defense attorney once argued that my name and phone was posted on my employer's website and I was likely a business owner and my phone number was scraped from the internet and therefore there were no violations of TCPA and the case should be immediately dismissed for lack of cause. He threatened to file a motion for summary judgment. The attorney was obviously not familiar with TCPA. I had met him before at a previous hearing and he informed me that he used to work a lot of traffic ticket business but it really did not pay the bills. I respected him because he had a law degree but was not impressed with his scope of work and background. In a hearing in which he was unprepared and being beaten mercilessly, he started babbling something so strange I could not decipher what he was saying. It was so incoherent I began to wonder if the poor guy was having a stroke. The words were not just disjointed but illogical as to the sentence structure. It was pure gibberish. The judge looked at me and asked if I would like to respond. I replied, "I don't have a clue as to what he is talking about and I will stand with my arguments." She obviously agreed. Maybe she knew what he was doing, but I had no clue.

When later telling an attorney about the actions by the attorney he expl
When attorneys are losing so egregiou
factual or emotional arguments on wh
they are trained to deflect with rand
the discussion in another direction an
argument. I later thought of it as being hilarious. It was one of my first arguments in front of a judge and I was not only prepared but overly prepared. I had to be; the judge did not want to hear the case and I knew it. But, I finally got to beat up my first attorney in court and it was a satisfying experience and it was enjoyed immensely with great pride. More importantly, the attorney had to call his client explaining how he lost the motion to a non-attorney. Gratification comes in many forms.

As to the phone number being posted on an employer's website and on my emails, I argued that defense could not find anywhere in law or in case law where this is considered consent to call. Millions of Americans do the same and they do not lose their constitutional rights to privacy. As a matter of fact, TCPA addresses residential phone lines, cellular phones including text messaging and unwanted junk faxes. Businesses can be called but if a business owner registers his or her cellular phone on the Do Not Call Registry, it is a violation to call. There is an entire industry that scrubs and updates phone lists daily for a nominal fee. A phone number being published somewhere on the internet does not authorize consent to call under TCPA. Don't be fooled. It is not a real argument.

Chapter 16:

Clear and Conspicuous Consent

Consent to call is legally required to be clear and conspicuous. I had a small case early in my adventures with a telemarketer. My family doctor gave me a discount coupon for a heart calcium screening. The cost was $79. I have great insurance but I just went to the medical provider and paid cash, got the screening and left. I had signed a few forms but was not concerned. I paid in advance for a simple service. There was no debt or bill to be paid at a later date. A few weeks later I started getting calls selling healthcare insurance from a local company. I repeatedly asked the caller to stop calling but they refused. After five calls, I filed a lawsuit with specific language set by statute regarding carve outs afforded the healthcare industry in regard to consent. The defendant hired legal counsel. The attorney was a 60-year-old man whow as new with a longtime, well-established law firm. He was the new guy and was assigned the small case. There was no discovery. I had phone records and I knew the identity of the defendant and the phone number they called from was publically published. I was waiting for the court to issue a trial date. Three or four months later the trial date was set. This spurred the sharing of discovery. Their attorney sent a document listing consent to call that I had signed. He had never mentioned it before. This was a form I had signed at the hospital for the heart screening test. On the back page, line 18 of 30, it clearly stated in small print that a debt collector, attorney or medical billing company could contact me telephonically. This was their excuse for the consent argument to have the case dismissed.

After doing some research on the caller I learned that they were a medical billing agent and a debt collector licensed with the state, but again, I had paid cash for the screening services and there was no debt to be collected. The disclosure of consent to call was neither clear nor conspicuous, prominently displayed or verbally disclosed while signing the documents.

The hospital was obviously selling my name to a marketing service and I really did not care for their deception. It is a large, well-known regional healthcare service provider, a major hospital. I was not happy. I trusted that a hospital would treat my personal information with great prudence. I was wrong; they shared it with others. I later found that this is common practice. I considered finding others that were similarly situated and could qualify as a potential class action case. I thought maybe they assumed that I was uninsured. I supposed that the size of the class members would be too small and decided against it and just moved on with the case as is. I sent their attorney the actual language used in case law regarding clear and conspicuous consent and he begrudgingly had his client agree to settle. It was a small case but the defendant's attorney tried to bully me because I was a pro se filer. It was only five calls and I was paid statutory damages and went about my business.

Here is a comment regarding special offers, promotions, sweepstakes and entries for prizes. I have not filled out, signed up for, or authorized anyone to call me for over a decade. It is only inviting unwanted nuisance calls and you may or may not have a legitimate cause of action. The money to be made in the give away promotions is in the list itself. It is for sale and will be used against you. The downside is that I will not win the Publishers Clearing House grand prize.

I suggest readers register on the National Do Not Call Registry if they have not already done so. It will not stop unwanted calls. This will only add value when filing a lawsuit and naming the specific violation in a complaint.

Limiting social media can be helpful. I do not have a Facebook account but I have used LinkedIn for business purposes. I do not accept invitations just because I receive an email stating that someone would like to join my network. I have not seen a case in which the caller argued an established relationship from the acceptance of an internet based contact but I think it could possibly be a valid defense.

Here is an example of how you may get on a call list. Let's say you want to know today's price of silver. You go online and search for today's prices. Some website providers will capture your IP address. From there, they think you are a potential precious metals buyer. They can then correlate your name, address, phone number and email. The information can be sold to a lead provider who can spam you with pop-up ads, emails and even phone calls. Just because you checked the price of silver, it does not mean that they have consent to call, but some will. Once you are on a call list you may never get off. I let them keep calling until there were enough calls to make it worth my time to file a lawsuit.

If you ever need a little extra cash, just start searching today's price of silver or gold. They will call.

I do not block call numbers for two reasons. I do not know how and, if I did, I still would not do so. It is giving away free money and the caller would likely change their spoof number anyway.

Chapter 17:

Vicarious Liability, the "Not Me" Defense

This is important. Often defendants will argue that they did not actually make the calls. It is pretty common for defendants to deny any and all allegations of telemarketing violations but frequently the defendant will state that they hired a third party telemarketer and therefore they are not liable for the calls and the lawsuit should be dismissed. THEY ARE WRONG. Do not let this become a roadblock. Sometimes the defendant will redirect the plaintiff by naming the actual caller or telemarketing firm to avoid litigation. Occasionally they will even supply contracts, invoices and emails identifying the true telemarketer. Filing a lawsuit solely against the telemarketing firm has many pitfalls such as them folding up shop or filing for bankruptcy. They will have another corporation already registered, set up and ready to go back into business, restarting their telemarketing activities the very next day. They are prepared because they know they are violating federal law but do not want to interrupt their income stream. It happens.

Some defendants go on to state in their answer to the complaint that the plaintiff should be responsible for all costs of the defendant's legal representation. I have never experienced a court to consider such a request. If the plaintiff can identify the defendant and their actions and has a valid claim supported by evidence and a legitimate cause of action there should be no issue.

At times they claim that they are just a lead buyer but there are very definite distinctions between a lead buyer and a defendant that has a direct relationship with a telemarketer.

The law reads as follows:

****

"The TCPA imposes vicarious liability on third-parties who do not physically dial the calls."

****

The law continues to read as follows:

****

Under the TCPA, a seller of a product or service may be vicariously liable for a third-party marketer's violations of Sections 227(b) and 227(c), even if the seller did not physically dial the illegal call, and even if the seller did not directly control the marketer who did. In re Joint Pet filed by Dish Network, LLC, FCC 13-54 ¶ 37, 2013 WL 193449 (May 9, 2013) ("FCC Ruling").

****

The Dish Network cases combined produced total damages and penalties that exceeded $300 million and delivered rulings even further the exacting of the definitions of vicarious liability.

In reaching her decision, Judge Myerscough rejected Dish's contention that the majority of the calls were made by third party vendors or retailers that the company had little to no control over.

The additions to vicarious liability definitions now include the following:

****

Additionally, a seller may be vicariously liable for violations of those provisions under principles of apparent authority and ratification. Factors relevant to a finding of vicarious liability include:

a. Whether "the seller allows the outside sales entity access to information and systems that normally would be within the seller's exclusive control, including . . . access to detailed information regarding the nature and pricing of the seller's products and services or to the seller's customer information."

b. Whether the outside sales entity can "enter consumer information into the seller's sales or customer systems."

c. Whether the outside sales entity has "the authority to use the seller's trade name, trademark and service mark."

d. Whether "the seller approved, wrote or reviewed the outside entity's telemarketing scripts," and

e. "Whether the seller knew (or reasonably should have known) that the telemarketer was violating the TCPA on the seller's behalf and the seller failed to take effective steps within its power to force the telemarketer to cease that conduct."

****

Vicarious liability has arisen on multiple occasions. One case in particular comes to mind. A company that I sued lied and denied as to all allegations in their original answer to the complaint. This is standard operating procedure for some. Given I was a Pro Se filer, they thought that they could get away with their digressions as to the law and truthful responses. The case was filed and served. A discovery was approved by the lower court and the defendant produced a Third Party Sales Agreement with a telemarketing firm operating and calling out of the Philippines.

The agreement was a ten-page document meant to protect the defendant. It was a work of art crafted by a highly skilled attorney that supposedly made an ironclad agreement that vanquishes any and all liability of the defendant. The defendant proclaimed that they were merely a lead buyer and could not be held responsible for the actions of others. The agreement even stated that the Philippine Company was liable for any and all TCPA violations and should operate within the confines of US law. At issue was jurisdiction. There is no jurisdiction for US companies to sue Filipino companies that I am aware of, nor do they have to comply with subpoenas for phone records. Suing the Filipino company would have been fruitless.

A small section of the Agreement read as follows:

"The permitted use by the telemarketer of the (defendant's name) shall be subject to the instruction and restriction of 'The Company' in The Company's sole discretion. All material containing The Company's name shall be reviewed and approved by The Company prior to the ISO using them."

This proved my case, and the defendant provided the weapon and the ammunition.

In short, there was additional proof that the defendant instructed the telemarketing company, allowed the use of the company's trade name, input consumer information and approved telemarketing sales scripts. This is exactly what the judicial opinion wrote in the Dish Network case. The most brazen lie was that the signer of the agreement was an independent outside agent. He was actually an employee of the defendant company, or at least that is what his Facebook page indicated.

In all, there was a tremendous number of provable lies and untruths stated in the answer to the complaint, in discovery and in a signed and notarized affidavit by the CEO. The CEO was named personally in the lawsuit. Once there was proof of all the evidence and blatant lies, he was convinced to settle. He did not want the court and a jury to hear any of the evidence. He knew he was toast.

The defendant paid treble damages but escaped a federal class action law suit because the Philippines is outside the jurisdiction of the US and the subpoena for phone records as proof violations would not occur.

A choice can be made as to whom you wish to sue, the telemarketer and/or the selling company or both. Sometimes it depends on the financial status of the defendant(s). I have never been afraid of going after large corporations and I prefer to oppose attorneys rather than company management or executive staff. It is easier, they are less emotional and attorneys better understand the law and consequences. They are more likely to resolve the issue rather than going to court.

For anyone who knows attorneys,most are not litigators and dread being in a court room, especially in front of a jury. Besides, their clients don't want to pay their fees. In most cases it is less expensive to settle. It is just a matter of how much and when.

Either way, vicarious liability is real, and there is no escape clause for those who hire telemarketers and do not actually make the calls. They can legally be held liable.

Chapter 18:

Jurisdiction

The term jurisdiction can be applied in a variety of fashions with totally different meanings. The greater percentage of the lawsuits filed had out-of-state defendants. Defendants often assert that the claim lacks jurisdiction. In other words, they deny doing business in the state in which the plaintiff resides, claiming that they conduct no business within the state and so on. The statements are obviously false and are easily provable once phone records are obtained. The nearly universal rule is that the courts in a state have jurisdiction over all people or businesses that are citizens of or do business in that state.

The following is included in the original compliant:

Plaintiff is a resident of XXXX County (State). The Defendant is a company that solicits business in the State of XXXX and has an office located in (defendant's city and state).

Chapter 19:

Personal Jurisdiction

Personal jurisdiction gives a court the authority to make decisions binding on the persons involved in a civil case. This comes into play when an individual such as CEO or company president is named and served in a lawsuit personally as well as their company.

Some companies have filed bankruptcy to avoid the expense of lawsuits in higher courts. In a few cases, the defendant declared upfront that they would file for bankruptcy to nullify any monetary awards that the court may render in its decision. This is often a negotiation tactic but at times it is a genuine concern due to the amount of potential damages. The mistake made is that if only the corporation was named in the lawsuit, the company can be dissolved. By naming individuals personally responsible for and participatory in the decisions of the company regarding illegal telemarketing activities, they would have to personally file for bankruptcy as well. If the defendant company actually files for bankruptcy, all that is left is a defunct business with no ability to pay. This leaves the plaintiff with only the satisfaction of putting a bad guy out of business. The defendant is forced to start anew and spend thousands with a bankruptcy attorney. When company directors are named personally they are likely to be more willing to at least negotiate a settlement. They do not want personal assets at risk. In later cases, with lessons learned, I began naming the principals of the company, presidents, CEO's, etc. There must be evidence of their participation or a reasonable probability that they contributed to or authorized the prohibited acts. It costs a little extra to have them served but it is worthwhile. On some occasions the individuals were named in the original petition and others later when the original petition was amended with the court's approval.

Company executives or owners scream with contempt when they are named personally as a defendant. When the company executive is personally named in the lawsuit and once a judgment has been rendered in the plaintiff's favor, the executive knows their individual assets may be at stake as well as the corporation. This gets their attention; now it becomes personal. They start to take it seriously.

In this situation, expect the defendant to hire local counsel to file a motion for a hearing with written arguments regarding lack of personal jurisdiction to have their client removed from the complaint as an individual. The plaintiff will have to make arguments to the presiding judge to avoid the defendant escaping personal liability.

I have argued this using precedent-setting cases to make my point and have not lost on this particular issue to date. Forgive the legalese of the following as it may be necessary to know case history and how to overcome the defense's motion.

The cases of precedent are as follows:

Case One

Individual Defendants discuss in their Motion, the court in Texas v. American Blastfax, Inc., 164 F.Supp.2d 892 (W.D. Tex. 2001), has set forth and explained the standard for officer liability in the arena of the Telephone Consumers Protection Act (the "TCPA"). **The court stated that, as a general matter, an officer may be personally liable for a violation of a federal** statute "if the officer directly participated in or authorized the statutory violation, even though acting on behalf of the corporation." The court went on to Case 4:17-cv-00289-ALM-KPJ Document 26 Filed 10/10/17 Page 3 of 9 PageID #:133 say specifically, with regard to the TCPA, that "an officer may be personally liable under the TCPA if he had direct, personal participation in or personally authorized the conduct found to have violated the statute, and was not merely tangentially involved." The court concluded that "individuals who directly ... violate the TCPA should not escape liability solely because they are corporate officers[;] ... to hold otherwise, would allow the individual defendants to simply dissolve [the offending corporation], set up a new shell corporation, and repeat their conduct." Id. "Congress surely did not intend to permit such a result in passing the TCPA."

Case Two

Creative Montessori Learning Center v. Ashford Gear, LLC, Jack Burns, and Brian Reeves Case # 09 C 3963 in the District Court for Northern District of Illinois, Easter Division.

In summation, the court ruled that those who are merely shareholders or investors but not in control of daily operations even though they personally benefit from these actions are not subject to personal jurisdiction but **those who are in direct control of day-to-day activities are held to personal jurisdiction.**

Case Three

3.) Larry v. Doctors Answers, LLC, No. cv-12-S-3510-NE, 2013 WL 987879 (N.D. Ala. March 8, 2013)

An Alabama Plaintiff sued New Jersey Defendants for violating the TCPA by sending an unsolicited fax advertising material for answering services provided by Defendant. Defendant filed a Motion to Dismiss challenging Personal Jurisdiction, Venue and Plaintiff's ability to state a claim upon which relief can be granted. The court denied the motion on all grounds.

With respect to Defendant's challenge to the court's personal jurisdiction, the court recited the United States Supreme Court's express acknowledgement that "'federal interest in regulating telemarketing to protect the privacy of individuals while permitting legitimate commercial practices' 'would be less well served if consumers had to rely on 'the laws or rules of court of a State' or the accident of diversity jurisdiction, to gain redress for TCPA violations.' Thus, 'federal courts [have] federal-question jurisdiction over private TCPA suits.'"

The opinion went on to state the following regarding personal jurisdiction: The corporation is liable under the doctrine of "respondeat superior." **It does not relieve the individuals of their responsibility, adding that "an officer may be personally liable under the TCPA if he had direct, personal participation in or personally authorized the conduct found to have violated the statute, and was not merely tangentially involved. Individuals who directly (and here, knowingly and willfully) violate the TCPA should not escape liability solely because they are corporate officers."**

Case Four

Vicarious Liability and Respondeat Superior

In Miller v. Merchants Credit Adjusters, Inc., 2015 WL 4205159 (D.Neb.,2015), Judge Bataillon allowed a TCPA Plaintiff to amend his complaint to add the principals upon whose behalf a debt was being collected because, as the Court explained, the TCPA permits respondeat superior theories.

"While section 227(b) does not contain a provision that specifically mandates or prohibits vicarious liability, we clarify that the prohibitions contained in section 227(b) incorporate the federal common law of agency and that such vicarious liability principles reasonably advance the goals of the TCPA."

In Bridgeview Health Care Ctr. Ltd. v. Clark, 2013 WL 1154206, at *4–5 (N.D.Ill. Mar. 19, 2013) **("[T]he TCPA creates a form of vicarious liability making an entity liable when a third party sends unsolicited communications on its behalf in violation of the [TCPA]."). "Under the doctrine of respondeat superior, an employer is held vicariously liable for the negligent acts of an employee committed while the employee was acting within the scope of the employer's business."**

******

This is a lot of legal jargon, but winning a personal jurisdiction hearing can be the difference in winning, settling a case and getting paid. There are likely many more cases of precedent. Readers who face this issue should research case law if confronted with this defense strategy. The other alternative is having an uncollectable paper judgment due to a defendant's business bankruptcy. You can always frame the judgment and display it on a wall but the value will be in the frame. Winning a personal jurisdiction hearing can also expedite the settlement of a case. Corporate executives never want their personal assets put in jeopardy. It depends on the defendant and their attitude towards pro se filers and as to what amount of risk they are willing to take. Defense attorneys do not like being beaten by non-attorneys and they like it even less when they have to inform their clients that they lost the argument in court and the motion was denied. In one case it infuriated the defense counsel to the degree that he would not make an offer until the week of the trial.

There have been a few cases in which the defendant did not answer or defend the lawsuit. I was left to file for a default judgment, prove my case to the court and chase down the money through bank levies. I saw no reason to attempt to collect a judgment using normal collection practices. There would be no calls or letters in an attempt to collect. This only opens the door for settlement negotiations or heated conversations. Any advanced warning or threats of a bank levy would probably unleash actions of bank account withdrawals in an effort to hide the cash. When the bank levy is legally imposed, the defendant's bank account is frozen, and the balance is no longer accessible. The defendant will receive a letter from their bank and/or checks will begin to bounce. They may want to negotiate at this time depending on the balance of the account(s) at the time of the levy. Leave this up to legal professionals, as laws and procedures vary from state to state.

Chapter 20:

Article III Standing and Injury in Fact

Over the years many defendants have challenged that concrete injury and harm had not occurred, the plaintiff lacked standing and the case should be dismissed. In layman's terms, the argument is basically, "It was a phone call, what actual harm was done?" In many cases the courts have agreed and dismissed cases for lack of standing. This is a complex issue with a great deal of legal background. TCPA provides statutory damages established by congress. To void damages due to lack of standing would in effect nullify TCPA. Yet in many courts, justices have done just that. A few years ago defense attorneys howled with delight as to a Supreme Court ruling in the case of Spokeo v Robins. This was not a TCPA case but privacy rights and the subject of concrete harm was addressed. Since this was a Supreme Court decision, there was great talk that telemarketing violators would once again have free reign to act in violation of federal law without repercussion due to the issue of standing. Shortly after came the case of Holderread v Ford Motor Credit. The judge had quite a challenge in front of him given the Spokeo case and the court's opinion regarding standing. Judge Mazzant of the Eastern District Court of Texas stated that when Congress enacted the TCPA to protect consumers' privacy rights, it "identified the intangible harm of invasion of privacy as legally cognizable."

This is only the judge's opinion in part, but it is powerful. Other courts have agreed. I have never had a defendant motion for dismissal for lack of standing and it is always included in the complaint.

There is another obstacle that many face today in regards to standing. Many have phone services billed to a family member or to their employer. In the case of Leyse v Bank of America, the case was originally dismissed by a district court because the called party (Leyse) shared a residential line with his roommate and the calls were not intended for him but for his roommate. The case was dismissed due to lack of statutory standing.

The case was appealed to the United States Court of Appeals, Third Circuit. The court recognized that the term "called party" was not limited to the intended recipient. The FCC in a declaratory order defined the "called party" as the "subscriber" or "customary user" of the phone number.

For those who are in the predicament of receiving countless unwanted calls on your company supplied phone or when you are not the listed subscriber, you may have a legitimate standing to file a lawsuit against those who invade your privacy.

In the case of those who use a company supplied phone, the issue may become the employer's permission and release of phone records. Phone users have the right to their own phone records but this could be a delicate matter.

Sometimes phone companies will go to great lengths to avoid the issue and attempt not to deliver. Often phone companies' customer service staff will state that the records can only be released by subpoena. This is not true unless you are attempting to obtain the records of others. At times it can be the matter of an untrained customer service representative and others a blatant attempt to withhold. I have experienced delay and stall tactics, the promise of delivery with no results and forced to repeatedly call back time and again and get the same results—nothing. In one instance I was sent the phone records of another individual after several calls and requests. Maybe they thought that they would appease me or maybe they were just inept.

I called the phone company compliance department in New York and was told under no circumstances was I allowed to receive my phone records without a subpoena. She also clearly stated it was company policy and a FCC regulation. I argued that the company had authorized the same request multiple times in the past and there was no such regulation and she would not have the ability to prove it because it did not exist. She demanded with great authority that this was company policy and there was no further need for discussion. I replied to her statement by saying, "the only way to obtain a subpoena is by court order and to my knowledge the only way to get an order was by filing a lawsuit in federal court, so who am I going to sue, your company? You cannot tell me that an individual has to file a lawsuit in federal court to obtain their own phone records." Then I reminded her that I had received the phone records of another individual and that he likely had mine. This got her attention. She probably knew that this was true because all of my previous calls were logged and she was looking at the records on her computer screen.

Once she realized what had been done, she wanted the records back immediately. They were sent in error and violated the other person's privacy rights as well as mine. This could become a substantial issue if the other party was made aware and I was in possession of his name and phone number. All I had to do was to call the other party. The phone company rep demanded that I return the phone records. Finally, realizing I had leverage, I stated that once I receive my records you will receive yours. The records were sent overnight delivery and were here the next morning before 10 am. Unfortunately, the process took over a month and several phone calls. I cannot be certain as to their motives but the defendant, a notorious telemarketer, was also their customer and made thousands of calls per day. The point is that the public has the right to their own phone records and sometimes it takes a little persistence. My experience is that cell phone records are much easier to obtain by going online and downloading the information.

Chapter 21:

The Letter of Intent to File a Lawsuit

A letter of intent to sue is exactly what it sounds like. It is a formal written notice of the intent to file a lawsuit if the issue is not resolved within a specific period of time. This is putting the defendant on notice and granting them an opportunity to respond prior to litigation and avoid the cost of doing so.

There are several good reasons to send a letter of intent to file a lawsuit. It is not legally required but valuable information can be gained on occasion. This tactic is best used in smaller cases. Larger cases are just served with a lawsuit. I don't always do this but at times it is helpful.

In a number of instances, it was a waste of time. The respondent did not answer. There is nothing lost other than a few weeks and the cost of certified mail. If they refuse to respond, do not call them, file the lawsuit and have them served. Then, they will be required to respond or face a default judgment.

Sometimes, especially in smaller cases, an attorney will call or write and resolve the issue by simply paying. They know their client violates federal law and they want to minimize the damages and their client does not want to incur legal expenses to defend. They will send a settlement agreement to be signed followed by a check. It is up to the plaintiff to negotiate the amount of the check and date and method of delivery of payment and should be clearly specified in the agreement.

Now and then I am just looking for an actual address or other unknown information. Other times I am hoping for additional evidence or weak legal arguments in the response. If the certified letter is returned undelivered, there is a need to dig deeper. Many corporations will have a Registered Agent on file with the Secretary of State. Each state has a website disclosing all corporations registered within their state. The Registered Agent is designated to receive service of process or other legal documents on behalf of the defendant. Some defendants go to great lengths to disguise their true location. Postage for the letter of intent is more cost effective than filing a lawsuit and paying a process server.

If writing as a pro se, attorneys may hold you in low regard and might not take your claim seriously. Sometimes they may carelessly respond with a letter that includes actual details and information that you may be unaware of. The information may be helpful to your cause and give the ammunition needed to move forward with the claim. A few have named third party telemarketing firms with which they work. I have experienced them handing over invoices, written agreements and emails which can prove the case against them and their telemarketing counterparts.

In one case I was told that I could either take a cheap settlement or be rolled into a larger class action. I took the money. Class members of a class action lawsuit usually get almost nothing. Attorneys get the majority of funds and the lead plaintiff is paid to some degree and class members get the scraps that are left over. In this case I was paid $500 but all I spent was the cost of a certified letter. The mistake made was the lack of research. I did not find the class action case was already filed against the defendant. My information could have been valuable to the lead plaintiff's attorneys and maybe I could have contributed with evidence that would have solidified their case, but I did not want to become a class member to receive a few dollars. It happens.

Defendants will also attempt to make legal arguments that really do not exist, can be easily overcome or are irrelevant to the case. Knowing this is their only defense, they will lose and it is helpful in crafting your complaint to the court. It's a nice feeling.

Evidence is not provided in the letter of intent other than stating facts such as dates, times, spoof numbers used, identifying verbiage used during the sales call or other relevant information to the case. There is no supporting documentation attached. The defendant already has all of the call records and possibly voice recordings. It is their choice to either confirm or deny the allegations.

In some cases there is complete denial. Some defendants have even denied telemarketing altogether. This is when a little research pays off. In more than one case I emailed defense counsel a screenshot or printouts of the defendant's help wanted ad for telemarketers or appointment setters. I did not know if his client was lying to him or he was lying to me, but someone was definitely lying. If this was presented to a jury it would give them one less defense argument and a lot less credibility. Defense attorneys do not like seeing proof of their lies and it usually results in a fairly hostile response.

If they want evidence such as phone records, they will make the request. Once proven, dialogue can begin.

In one case, the defendant answered the letter of intent but not to the lawsuit. The attorney's written response was helpful in later obtaining a default judgment against the defendant.

The letter of intent was sent by me as a non-attorney, the case was filed in federal court with attorney representation seeking a class action. Again, sometimes defense attorneys think the majority of the American public grew up a little too close to the high voltage powerlines and lack the superior intellect they possess.

This particular attorney and others have made the same threats mentioned in an earlier chapter alleging extortion, blackmail and countersuits with financial ramifications to me. Again, I recognize it as standard operating procedure. The only significant effect regards my willingness to settle and their costs to defend. They always pay for their digressions and attempts to intimidate.

The actual letter of intent includes items such as defendant and plaintiff name and address, date, the verbiage that this is a formal notice of my intent to file a lawsuit for violations of TCPA and the location of the court where the complaint will be filed. The court location to be filed puts them on notice that it could be costly to defend since most are located out of state and they will need to hire local legal representation.

The letter also states the nature of the calls, the exact dates and times, spoof numbers used, receiving call number, defines cellular or residential phone line called, verbiage used by the caller and products or services sold. I also recite legal language as well as statutory damages and verbiage about willing and knowing acts for treble damages and amount of relief requested. I give the defendant fourteen days to respond. The letter always ends with "if you do not respond within fourteen days from the date of receipt of this document I will initiate a lawsuit." If they do not respond, file the lawsuit.

On one occasion the defendant's attorney called about three weeks later. He started by wanting to discuss the serious allegations leveled against his client. He was told that the deadline had passed and the lawsuit had already been filed. This was not the response he was expecting. Maybe he assumed that I would call begging and groveling for a few bucks and he could verbally batter a non-attorney with legal arguments and intimidation. He was wrong; I never make the first call and I don't beg. He told me that he had been very busy and that I could have called him. I replied that I had no idea of who he was and that he should have taken the letter more seriously. He was not pleased. He was informed that his client should be served within the week he could answer the lawsuit. I also stated that next time he should be more prompt in his response. For some reason the call was abruptly ended but not by me. I got a chuckle.

Chapter 23:

Attorneys

Attorneys can be invaluable in many ways, if not a necessity. My only wish is that more included TCPA as an area of practice. Finding one to represent a small case plaintiff is nearly impossible, even in large cities. Some attorneys are hungry enough, not well established and are not employed by big name law firms and will take almost any case brought to them. These are the types that are willing to learn and take on your cause. The important question is; are they paper pushers or litigators? A litigator is someone who is adept at trial and willing to stand in front of a jury and fight for your cause. The majority of attorneys never want to see the inside of a court room or face a jury.

In earlier cases, a good attorney would have saved a lot of time and trouble, but I would not have gained the knowledge that I have today. In years long passed, I had hired a few attorneys, but only once did I agree to an hourly rate. It resulted in my hard earned money and time being wasted and ended in the termination of our agreement. Many in the legal profession are adept at taking money and realizing no results, no communication and no returned phone calls. I have also learned over the years to allow them time, do not bother them, let them do their work and know the legal system is not oriented towards timely results and customer service. If you are working with an attorney and you don't hear from them in a month or two, send an email for a brief update and make the questions short and specific. Sometimes they need a bit of a push to get them back to work. But, I also follow the cases online and usually do not require a great deal of attention. Most attorneys have multiple clients and cases that they are working on simultaneously and will appreciate the patience. They will call when they have something of importance to say. A good relationship with an attorney that is well versed in TCPA is of great value so respect it if you wish it to continue. Besides, they want to get paid too.

Today, all of my legal endeavors with attorneys are under a contingency agreement. If the attorney prevails, he or she is paid a percentage of the award. Under one agreement I pay the cost of court and under another I do not and the percentage paid reflects the difference.

Their expertise can make a dramatic difference in outcomes and the amount of damages awarded. A good attorney will command the attention and respect of your opponent which may not be the case of a pro-se filer. An attorney that practices in the area of TCPA will keep up to date on precedent-setting court cases, rulings and FCC regulations that may affect the outcome of your case. The law is forever expanding and new FCC rules are almost always in favor of the consumer.

I have experienced first hand a judge question the credibility of my testimony even when supported by the exact text stated in written law. When the same facts were presented by a licensed attorney, they seem to bear more weight and were considered as true.

At issue is that attorney fees are not allowed under TCPA. This can make smaller claims unworthy of an attorney's time. Most attorneys do not want small cases, because like the rest of us, they have to make a living. In the creation of TCPA, Senator Hollings wrote that it would defeat the purposes of the bill if the attorneys' costs to consumers of bringing an action were greater than the potential damages. This leaves many plaintiffs to go it on their own.

Three of four calls at $500 to $1,500 per call may not entice an attorney unless the case has the potential of becoming a class action lawsuit. Twenty, thirty calls or more may. This is especially important when applying TCPA to debt collection agency calls. There are often other violations of federal law in addition to TCPA. Many of these cases include infractions of the Fair Debt Collection Practices Act. I have not participated in this type of case but I know of those who have. They can be very profitable for all involved (except the defendant).

I still file cases pro se in lower courts, mostly because they are too small to justify my attorney's time and I do not want to share the awards. I have learned case by case, and never lost. Larger cases go through an attorney. I do not have the expertise, ability, legal training or time to attempt to fight in higher courts. The procedures and rules are way beyond my capacity. I must admit that I have learned a great deal from working with true professionals and even borrowed segments of their legal writings.

When hiring a legal counsel one must first present the case to the attorney to gain their interest. Have all of the documents needed and be able to establish your cause. Supply a copy of the Do Not Call registration. This is easily done by entering the www.donotcall.gov website and by clicking to verify your registration. Have phone records available as proof of the unwanted calls. Research the defendant's website and gather as much information as possible. Print off Secretary of State's Business entity lookup to prove that there is a legally viable defendant, if available. Provide a written detailed account of the actual phone calls. Include dates, times, spoofed phone number used, distinguish residential line or cellular phone called, prerecorded messages if applicable, verbiage used by the caller, any statements that you made during the call and all other information that is relevant to the case. If you have caught the attorney's interest, he or she will likely avoid making an immediate decision due to their analytical and skeptical nature. Request a response within a certain time frame so as not to allow your case file to sit on their desk like a dozen others.

Federal cases have all been filed with the intent of gaining class action status. These cases may well exceed the award limits of lower courts due to the sheer volume of calls. In this type of case, the lead plaintiff is representing all others that received unwanted marketing calls and those on the Do Not Call Registry, without consent to call or other violations depending on the circumstances of the case.

While usually done with lower court cases in a matter of months, class actions can take several months or even a few years or more to finalize. Then again, sometimes settlement offers come more quickly because there is a lot at stake for the defendant. If successfully settled, the attorney will be paid a percentage of the settlement if an agreement is reached prior to the finalization of the case through the court system. In class action cases in which the case is finalized and the court awards in favor of the plaintiff(s), attorney's fees are allowed. The amount paid to the attorney will be submitted to the court for their approval.

Chapter 24:

Class Action Lawsuits

Class action cases are a matter of federal jurisdiction only, meaning they can only be filed in the federal court system. They require a highly skilled attorney. Attorney fees are allowed in class action cases if class status is granted by the court and the plaintiff prevails. These attorneys are a rare breed but are more easily found to some degree. These are high dollar cases and there are counselors who practice specifically in this area of the law.

Class action cases can be complicated but potentially extremely profitable for the lead plaintiff. Four, five or twenty-five calls can lead to millions in damages paid and expenses for the defendant if class action status is granted by the court. I am still dumbfounded that some defendants believe that violating TCPA comes with a risk of $500 per call that will be settled quickly and cheaply prior to even answering the lawsuit. I recently experienced a case in which the defendant's marketing guru response to a federal class action lawsuit was to see if he could make an offer of a quick settlement. In an email he wrote that he would discuss the matter with company hierarchy and get an answer right away. The gentleman came back with a solid offer of $500. The cost of filing the lawsuit and process of service was nearly $500. He seemed offended and frustrated in a follow-up email that there was no response or even a counter offer. The exact verbiage used in his email was "What, not even a counter offer?" Hopefully, he finally realized that this was not a small claims case in the local court system that could be swept under the rug and would quickly disappear.

Damages are $500 to $1,500 per call in this particular case. What the defendant did not realize is that if a class action was certified, they could be financially responsible for the identification and, more importantly, the expense of the notification of the potential class members. This could mean notifying possibly hundreds of thousands or more of those who were called. This process can add up to tens or hundreds of thousands of dollars of court ordered expenses depending on the size of the class, not to mention other legal expenses incurred just to defend.

As many may know, in class action lawsuit the real winners are the attorneys. In a recent case, the defendant paid $18,000,000 in damages. The class members received $25 each and the attorney fees were limited by the court not to exceed $7,000,000.

There is a distinct difference between a class member and a lead plaintiff. Class members are only those who were later identified and notified and opted to join the lawsuit already in progress
.

The lead plaintiff is the person who initiated the lawsuit. The lead plaintiff is representing those that may be similarly situated and are included in the lawsuit as class members.

The lead plaintiff can be awarded an amount determined by the court. The lead plaintiff has responsibilities as to hiring the attorney(s), consulting on the case, assisting with discovery, providing documents and evidence, participating in depositions, answering written and oral questions and has input as to approving or denying negotiated settlements. Only the lead plaintiff can object to a settlement. If the case is not settled, proceeds and finalizes through the court, the court may grant an award to the lead plaintiff based upon injuries suffered, size of the recovery and for the amount of participation in litigation and preparation. The amount can be substantial, and the court has broad discretion. At issue is that you want to be compensated for your time, efforts, skills and diligence. Attorneys can make recommendations to the court but the judge has the final decision.

BUT, there is another scenario to consider. Not all cases go to completion in the court system. Often there is a negotiated settlement to end the legal process. In one scenario, the defendant has denied all allegations and has spent tens of thousands on attorney fees to defend. A discovery deadline is approaching and the defendant knows they are guilty as hell and phone records will prove the fact and he is aware that things are about to go downhill quickly.

This is where the case just becomes interesting. Now the negotiations are based on the assumed size of the class or sometimes a percentage of the defendant's assets.(Please reread the last sentence as it changes the entire dynamics of the case and potential settlements.)At this point, there are no class members to consider because class certification has not been granted by the court. This can lead the negotiations that can well exceed the amount of the personal claim, thus the potential for a significant payout. It is the law, and it is the way things work. So, am I afraid of a class action? No, I welcome it with open arms.

Pay close attention to the last two paragraphs as it is extremely critical in achieving objectives and has potential for significant monetary gain. As in "Suttons Law," a notorious bank robber by the name of Willie Sutton was once asked by a reporter, why do you rob banks? Willie replied, "Because, that's where the money is." Just like Willie, this is where the money is. When you have a solid case, no matter the number of calls, have it reviewed by an attorney. If the attorney feels the defendant has deep enough pockets and there is presumed to be a sizeable prospective class, maybe you will have a much larger case than just the calls received. I wish I had learned this lesson earlier on in my endeavors but there are multiple cases pending with this exact scenario. This is a great option for those who do not want to get directly involved in the legal system and would like to see telemarketers prosecuted. If the readers only remember one thing, this is it.

Chapter 25:

Willing and Knowing Acts for Treble Damages

Courts may, at its discretion, increase damages up to three times the amount ($1,500 per call) for willing and knowing acts violating TCPA. I have filed cases, the defendant had been served and they still continued to call. If that is not a knowing and willing act, then I do not know what is. This happens far more often than one would think.

In earlier cases, I just hung up on callers and they continued to call. This is not a bad tactic to build the number of calls received and eventual damages. They will just continue to call until they want to stop. Some I told that I was on the Do Not Call list and continued to track their calls. Later, after filing an abundance of cases, I didn't really want more lawsuits, and if I did, I wanted them to be financially worthwhile. So, when called, I would state, "I sue telemarketers, I am on the DNC list and don't call again." Some stopped calling but I was surprised how many did not. They paid no attention whatsoever. My only guess is their employer had spent money to purchase a call list and they were not allowed to remove phone numbers. More likely the callers had a sales production and call quotas to fulfill with a limited number of prospects to contact. My other thought is that they really just didn't care and did not think they would be caught or sued. The motivation was twofold. One, maybe they will quit calling. Two, I could request relief for treble damages for all calls after the first because they were told on the very first call that I sue telemarketers. It was an easy way to allege willful conduct and seek relief of $1,500 per call. I knew it would play well in court and there would be more defendants worth suing.

I believe that spoofing a phone number is a willful and knowing act that qualifies for treble damages. This is an argument that I created that makes sense, at least to me. It was used when presenting a case to a judge and requesting maximum relief. This may or may not be considered in higher courts, but it has worked more than once in lower courts. To spoof a phone number that is displayed on the call recipients' caller ID function involves the purchase and download of spoofing software and the manual input of false phone numbers and caller ID names. This is an intentional and willing act.

Rarely does a case go to trial but juries almost always detest telemarketers or their unwanted calls. They will often recommend the maximum amount of penalties against the defendant.

The following is a recital of the knowingly and willingly portion of a plaintiff's complaint:

Courts may increase damages up to treble damages if the court finds that defendant's violations were committed "willfully or knowingly." 47 U.S.C. § 227(b)(3). Although neither the TCPA nor the FCC regulations define the terms "willfully or knowingly", courts have generally interpreted willfulness to imply only that an action was intentional. Smith v. Wade, 461 U.S. 30, 41 n.8 (1983). While the TCPA does not define willful, the Communications Act of 1943, of which the TCPA is a part, defines willful as **"the conscious or deliberate commission or omission of such act, irrespective of any intent to violate any provision",** rule or regulation." In Dubsky v. Advanced Cellular

Communications, Inc., No. 2008 cv 00652, 2004 WL 503757, at * 2 (Ohio Com. Pl. Feb. 24, 2004), **the court found that in the context of the TCPA, the term acting "Willfully" means that "the defendant acted voluntarily, and under its own free will, regardless of whether the defendant knew that it was acting in violation of the statute.**

In one Circuit Court, the judge wrote **"the intent for treble damages does not require any malicious or wanton conduct, but rather is satisfied by merely 'knowing' conduct."**

Always seek treble damages in the original complaint. The definitions of willful and knowing acts can easily be interpreted in the plaintiff's favor, irrespective of the defendant's knowledge of violating the law. Intentional, conscious, voluntary and deliberate acts may be determined by the court as willful or knowing. In some cases there is proof of previous lawsuits against the defendant for the same violations depicting a pattern of conscious illicit behavior.

In the interrogatories portion of discovery, I query the defendant if they are aware of TCPA. They can either confirm or deny. If the defendant admits knowledge of TCPA they may be subject to violations of knowing and willful acts and possibly liable for paying treble damages. Even knowing behavior, voluntary conduct and acting only of one's free will may be an accepted argument by the court with case history to support the claim. If the defendant claims knowledge of the law, it opens a can of worms regarding their misleading and deceptive actions of spoofing phone numbers, third party agreements, false names and websites used, verbiage used in their solicitations to avoid identity and much more. The question becomes, why would the defendant take these actions if there was no knowledge that they were in violation of federal law? The plaintiff or their counsel has great leverage to depict the defendant as having questionable character, to say the least. More importantly, their acts can justifiably be considered as willful, knowing and intentional. A skilled litigator can also question a witness on the stand, under oath and make them extremely uncomfortable when explaining their innocence to a jury. Either way, in the defendant's answers, there can be indications of behavior validating the plaintiff's claims.

Chapter 26:

Stackable Damages

An earlier chapter discussed TCPA banning the use of auto-dialers. There was a case in which the defendant called at least fifteen times that I could prove in court through phone records. The defendant was sued in federal court with the intent of gaining class action approval. The defendant decided not to answer the complaint leaving no other option but to file a motion for a default judgment. In later research, I found that the president of the company had just bankrupted another telemarketing company due to a class action lawsuit for the exact same violations.

The fifteen calls had statutory damages totaling $7,500 (up to $500 per call). The damages could be trebled to the amount of $22,500 for willingly and knowingly violating TCPA provision regarding the Do Not Call Registry. This is covered under 47 U.S.C. § 227(c)(5)(B). The complaint also alleged that the defendant used an auto-dialer. This is a separate violation that occurred within the same call. Each violation also had statutory damages of $500 and could treble to $1,500 per call for a total of another $22,500. This is covered under 47 U.S.C. § 227(b)(3). The total damages sought added up to $45,000 plus the cost of court. The separate violations occurred simultaneously within the same call. The precedent-setting case that is referred to in this section is Charvat v NMP LLC. The judge from the Sixth Circuit Court wrote in the opinion that damages can be awarded to the plaintiff for both violations even if both violations occurred within the same telephone call. The willingly and knowingly provision applied as well in both instances.

In Charvat v NMP LLC the judge's opinion reads as follows:

Charvat v. NMP, LLC, 656 F.3d 440, 449 (6th Cir. 2011)("We therefore conclude that a person may recover statutory damages of $1500 for a willful or knowing violation of the automated-call requirements, § 227(b)(3), and $1500 for a willful or knowing violation of the do-not-call-list requirements, § 227(c)(5)—even if both violations occurred in the same telephone call."); United States v. Dish Network LLC, No. 09-3073, 2017 WL 2427297, at *114 (C.D. Ill. June 5, 2017).

The defendant thought that he had only been liable for a total $7,500 for my specific claims but found out later it was much more. He did not answer the lawsuit because he thought it would be less costly just to pay. Telemarketers and the public should know this information. I hope those who choose to dial the phones with nuisance telemarketing calls get the message and rethink the invading of consumers' privacy.

On the consumer or plaintiff side, it is nice to know that there are violations where the courts can award up to $3,000 per call. Many cases will become worthwhile to pursue.

Chapter 27:

Judges

Judges' attitudes and behaviors regarding TCPA, privacy rights and even federal law seem to vary widely. This should not happen but it is a reality. Judges have an obligation to uphold the law and in the majority of instances, they do. As earlier mentioned, TCPA is a federal law in which Congress peculiarly authorized the right of private action in all courts including state run courts such as small claims. Plaintiffs can file a complaint in any court of their choosing. This often depends on the volume of calls being alleged, the damages calculated, the award limits of the court and the jurisdiction in which one resides.

Some lower court judges feel that TCPA has been forced upon them. They will rarely, if ever, hear a TCPA case and have almost no knowledge of this segment of the law other than the basics. Some do and some do not. Their first reaction is usually to read the rudiments of the law to determine if they even have to hear the case at all. Many judges are just like the American public; they have a searing loathing for telemarketers and their robocalls. Another interesting fact is that in many states, lower court judges are not required to have a law degree. These are elected officials that usually have a good grasp of state law in the limited scope of their daily work but not much beyond. Their true skills are that of campaigning, fund raising and politicking. Great detail must be presented in written and oral arguments so the judge can at least reference the exact letter of the law to support their findings. Hopefully, they will at least research the arguments, but it is not assured.

Some lower courts also dislike motions for discovery. Higher courts' judges see discovery as a matter of common practice that is established by rule without the begrudging consent often demanded with lower court judges.

A small percentage of judges see TCPA petitioners as nuisance filers attempting to exploit federal law to gain fast cash but hear cases only because it is a matter of federal law. Others take the invasion of consumers' privacy more seriously, as they should.

One case in particular comes to mind. I had filed several cases filed in a lower court over a few years' period. In only a few instances did I have to appear before the judge. Each time was for a discovery hearing that I had requested. All of the early cases were settled prior to trial and the judge really had little interaction with me or the defendant. Cases were filed, settled and she signed off on motions to dismiss with prejudice.

Then came a defendant that answered to complaint and hired a local attorney to argue personal jurisdiction. Personal jurisdiction came into play when I named and served the CEO of a company with a summons as well as his real company and the dummy company.

In short, I clearly won the hearing regarding the CEO's personal liability in the matter and the judge stated that there would be a decision by Friday. Well, dozens of Fridays have come and gone, motions for a court ruling, more supporting briefs have been filed and still no answer or a trial date have been issued.

I have motioned the court for a status conference in the past with the same results. The judge's statement: "I will have a decision by Friday," and the months pass on with no response.

A status conference is a polite way to ask the judge to get off of their ass and make a ruling so the case can move forward.

The judge did not want to hear the case and is retiring at the end of the year. She knew that I had filed several cases and had requested a few motions for discovery. Since the defendants had to hire an attorney and appear, the cases usually settled before they went through the expense to defend. On average, I was usually paid within a few months.

Another case pending in front of her court was one in which the defendant did not respond to the lawsuit and made no attempts to defend. I motioned the court for a default judgment hearing with a brief in support thereof containing the required information, federal law and precedent-setting case information required. The judge said, "I will have a decision by Friday." Once again, many Fridays came and went until I motioned the court for a status conference, which the court granted. In the hearing I regurgitated all of the same arguments given previously. The result was the same, "I will have a decision by Friday." I knew what that meant, so I waited. After a few more months went by, I finally received an award for default judgment letter in the mail. There was one catch. The court awarded $1,000. This was a clear signal that the judge never wanted me to file in her court again. The actual damages argued and supported by evidence, testimony and more could have reached $30,000 but I had only requested relief in the amount of $10,000 due to the limits of the lower court. The $1,000 was an insult and a clear message from the judge. If I would have known the judge was going to make such a small award I would have dismissed the case without prejudice and refiled in a higher court. I immediately filed a motion to reconsider, spelling out the exact letter of the law and it was instantaneously denied. I appealed. This judge did not want to hear this from a Pro Se filer and the court clerk displayed her displeasure with my actions. She made it as difficult as possible to complete the appeal bond documents to move the appeal forward. My guess is that the appeal questioned the judge's integrity and ability to fairly render a decision based in law. I had always been purposely polite and respectful with the judge and staff and this was pushing the limit, but I just smiled and gritted my teeth.

The appeal filed with the higher court (which I am sure the lower court judge read) and stated the following in a special comments section:

Comment: It is possible that the Telephone Consumer Protection Act (TCPA) can induce prejudice in lower courts due to manner in which it was created.

a) TCPA is unusual in that it allows for the right of private action in a state court but does not allow attorney fees. This often leaves Pro Se filers in Justice of the Peace Courts due to the plaintiff's lack of knowledge of court rules and procedures required in higher courts.

b) This also leaves lower court judges in the position of adjudicating cases for which they have little or no familiarity nor are they likely to hear a TCPA case but on extremely rare occasion or never. This places the justice in a difficult position to violate the Code of Judicial Conduct Section B (2) which states.... Adjudicative Responsibilities. (2) A judge should be faithful to the law and shall maintain professional competence in it.

c) TCPA is expansive and ever changing and would leave the justice great difficulties in maintaining competence in the law. Therefore, justices are in violation of the

(State) Code of Judicial Conduct. Thus prejudice or bias may occur and in TCPA cases. It is possible that the award of damages was lessened to deter future filings of a complaint and was not in adherence of the statutory damages established by congress.

Well, in short, this was not a brilliant move and neither judge appreciated my candor, but it sent a message. The appeals court judge never directly mentioned the special comments but made sure that I was put in my place with more than a few verbal lashings. I have never truly cared if I was liked or not but would rather be respected. Still yet, I had no interest in a $1,000 judgment, especially one that I was going to have to chase down to get paid. Besides, the lower court judge was retiring so I did not really care if she was offended. The only problem was that I have one last case pending in the lower court, so I had an attorney take over the case on a contingency fee basis. I literally had to find an attorney that was willing to be taught TCPA.

Today, I try to have cases filed in federal court with an attorney attempting to gain class action status. Federal judges seem to apply the law as it is written, which is not always true in lower courts. Taking on the case is left up to the attorney. Furthermore, when calculating the amount awarded, nearly eighty percent come from federal cases, but I still file in lower courts against smaller repeated violators that will not stop calling.

Chapter 28:

Serial Filer Claims

After filing a dozen or so TCPA lawsuits, I began to have concern about being labeled a serial filer or a professional plaintiff and that it may affect the outcome of my cases. I have heard of some individuals who have filed dozens of cases. There are others who have set up thirty telephone lines with the sole intent of catching telemarketers and filing TCPA lawsuits. The aforementioned case with the thirty phone lines was dismissed as frivolous. The plaintiff was verbally admonished by the court.

I thought my intentions were fairly straightforward. I would quit filing lawsuits when they stopped calling. I do not appreciate telemarketing calls and I think the abusers violate federal law daily with no concerns of repercussions whatsoever. I believe that I and others like me represent millions of consumers that cannot or will not fight back. More importantly, I was told in my first case that there was nothing I could do about it and since then I was forced to learn that I might as well use the knowledge for good. Throughout my business career I have probably lost a million or two by refusing to work with those who operate on the edge of the law. Maybe this is a way to even the score. Getting paid for my efforts has been a nice benefit.

Then I read a court opinion regarding a defendant who motioned the court for a dismissal claiming the plaintiff was a professional plaintiff. The defendant's counsel battered the plaintiff with accusations of being a professional plaintiff, listing all previously filed cases and social media postings. In fact, he was. He was one of the most active filers in the country as far as I know. The last I heard he had filed dozens of cases. The defendant went through the plaintiff's bank statements noting his lack of finances and that the plaintiff had written in social media that he enjoyed telemarketing calls and even looked forward to them. The defendant, in my opinion, was a serial caller. The defense had motioned the court for a dismissal due to the plaintiff's proven statements and behavior.

****

The judge in this case wrote the following in his decision: (the parties' names have been removed)

An ordinary consumer who pled the facts that (plaintiff) has pled would have established a concrete and particularized injury-in-fact based on the Defendants' intrusion upon his rights to privacy and seclusion. (See Doc. No. 57 at ¶ 78 (stating that Defendants infringed on plaintiff "right to be left alone")). Defendants suggest that, by becoming a so-called "professional plaintiff," he has forfeited those rights because the calls alleged were not truly unwanted.

It may be that plaintiff was not saddened or annoyed by the calls he received; it may even be that, knowing his rights under the TCPA, he is glad the calls were placed. But allowing that fact, even if true, to negate his right to privacy and seclusion would require the Court to embrace a line of reasoning that would ultimately undermine the rights of most, if not all, TCPA plaintiffs and plaintiffs in similar statutory schemes. The TCPA entitles a plaintiff to statutory damages in the generous amount of $500 per violation—a figure that can be tripled for a willful and knowing violation. 47 U.S.C. § 227(b)(3), (c)(5).

The Court ventures to guess that many ordinary people—not merely "professional plaintiffs"—would accept the fleeting invasion of their privacy associated with an unsolicited robocall for the reward of $1500—or even $3000, if more than one TCPA provision was violated.....If plaintiff has forfeited his right to privacy because he allegedly welcomed the calls, so too have those potential plaintiffs—or, at the very least, they lost their privacy rights the moment they understood they could sue to vindicate them. The Defendants seem to imagine a Constitution that limits the right to sue under the TCPA to those who are ignorant of their right to sue under the TCPA.

The Constitution requires no such result. The appropriate constitutional inquiry, rather, is whether a protected right was invaded, not whether the plaintiff subjectively considered the injury worth the eventual reward. The plaintiff, like every other private citizen, has rights to privacy and seclusion recognized by the law and protected from certain trespasses on those rights. The Court sees no authority for the proposition that his privacy interests ceased to exist merely because he realized that he could profit from suing for their invasion.

****

After reading the judge's opinion, I was somewhat relieved. Keep in mind the defendant was likely a notorious caller and probably lacked the innocence that they proclaimed.

At times I believe that my name has been registered on what I call "The Real Do Not Call List." Instead of averaging four to eight calls a day, I now receive six to ten calls a week. There are companies that screen for people like me because we do something about the unwanted calls. Others just complain and post their grievances on internet websites whining about their consumer rights and the laws to protect them or file FCC complaints. People like me file lawsuits and our names are recorded and published in public court records for all to see. Our names and phone numbers come with a special warning. The companies that scrub the Do Not Call list make it available to those who hire their services. More telemarketers should pay attention.

Chapter 29:

In Conclusion

Many say that our right to privacy is a thing of the past. Maybe that is true to some degree, but we do not always have to tolerate the nuisance of telemarketers and their unwanted calls. I hope this information will create havoc among the telemarketing industry and even put many of them out of business. Next time a friend or coworker complains about unwanted and unsolicited calls, give them a copy of this book and tell them to do something about it. Better yet, make it viral and share this with all.

Almost every argument and defense strategy that has been encountered has been addressed. To summarize the defense arguments will usually be based on consent to call, clear and conspicuous consent, hired third party callers under vicarious liability, jurisdiction, personal jurisdiction and standing. All can easily be overcome with established rules and case law.

Hopefully, some or maybe even many will start to sue those who choose to violate federal law and invade our privacy.

The way I originally viewed telemarketers was that there was $500 per call in damages and that it was payable to me. In my view, suing telemarketers killed two birds with one stone. I was constantly harassed by the calls and, of course, the $500 per call was like free money. All I had to do was take action.

From a purely business standpoint, it seemed to be a pretty good return on investment. There was money for the taking from those that I detested, and the calls were plentiful and free. In the first case I invested a little over a hundred dollars in court filing fees and the cost to have the defendant served. The end result is that I was paid over four thousand dollars. I cannot think of a better way to earn some extra cash without the significant investment of capital, time or the daily drudgery demanded by employers. It beats taking a part-time job and is far less time consuming. All that has to be done is to answer the phone, log the calls and do a little research.

An elderly family member was told of my escapades and he began asking questions about my new source of additional income. I did my best to answer but he did not seem to grasp the concept. He started by telling me of his business experiences throughout his life and asked how I obtained clients, and I replied, "they call me." He then asked, "well how do you get them to call? Do you advertise or is it word of mouth?" I replied, "no, they just call." He then asked if I built a rapport and attempted to establish a long-term relationship with my clients and of course I replied, no. He asked about the company and how I was treated. Do you get periodic performance reviews and are there opportunities for advancement? Do you have to fill out reports? Do you get a percentage of what you contribute to the business? The answers were all no. Then he asked with exasperation why people paid me money if I didn't even follow the basic principles of doing business. I responded, they don't pay me, I take their money, it's much easier that way, and that sales, building relationships, employers, reports and performance reviews had nothing to do with it. Again, I tried to explain and I'm not sure what information was comprehended but the conversation was changed, and we went on to other topics.
Filing TCPA lawsuits may appear overwhelming but the opposite is true. If I had possessed the knowledge earlier on

that I know today, I would have been compensated even more. The experiences discussed are an accumulation of three years of learning. It really did not take a great amount of my time and I enjoyed the challenges and the checks. I was getting paid to learn. At one point I estimated that I was making a pretty hefty three figure hourly rate for my labors. I definitely was not wasting my time. In time, with previous legal writings to use as a sample template, I could put together a letter of intent in twenty minutes and craft an original petition to file a lawsuit within an hour or two. As one gains experience, everything becomes easier and less time-consuming.

In reading this, you may have a better basic understanding of TCPA than many legal professionals. Of course they will have a much better foundation in knowledge of the law and court procedure and their industry should be highly respected.

I am not an attorney or a writer and maybe not exceptionally bright by most established standards. The traits that one may possess to be successful could include a profound dislike for telemarketing calls, stubbornness, a disregard for authority, intolerance of being pushed around, a willingness to investigate, a dislike for failure, enjoying a good fight, confidence, the ability to say no, and indifference as to how one is perceived by opponents and the lack of need for their approval.

In a final note to the readers, next time you receive an unwanted call, look at it as an opportunity instead of a nuisance. My goal is to arm the average American citizen with knowledge and to help them become the worst living nightmare that the telemarketing industry can imagine. Make all of my hopes and dreams come true.

I wish you good luck and good hunting.

Disclaimer:

The title of the book is *Killing Telemarketing*. Telemarketing should be considered as an industry and not as an individual. The writing does not refer to telemarketers personally. Many callers are just employees and in many cases they are oblivious to the law and even to their employer's actions. In some cases, they have no clue as to who they really work for. No one should hold any animus towards these folks. They are just trying to make a living. As to the author, he is not licensed to practice law or convey legal opinions. The writing is the result of personal experiences in legal actions but should not be considered as legal advice. The author cannot assist or advise in any legal undertaking.

Made in the USA
Middletown, DE
28 March 2019